Little Red Ridi...

A pantomime

Paul Reakes

Samuel French — London
New York - Toronto - Hollywood

LITTLE RED RIDING HOOD

First presented by the Timsbury Theatre Group at the Conygre Hall, Timsbury, Somerset, with the following cast:

Rosie Rumple—Red Riding Hood	Jo Day-Lewis
Roxie Rumple	Dennis Jones
Reggie Rumple	Brian Paterson
Grannie Grabbit	Maria Armstrong
Gertrude	Gaynor Mollard
Count De Cash	Peter Buchanan
Cringe	Ian Clark
Cower	Roger Bird
Prince Rupert	Julie Pow
Sternum	John Mulvey

Directed by **Jacki Watts**

CHARACTERS

Rosie Rumple—Red Riding Hood
Roxie Rumple, Rosie's mother
Reggie Rumple, Rosie's brother
Grannie Grabbit, Rosie's grandmother
Gertrude
Count De Cash
Cringe and **Cower**, the Count's footmen
Prince Rupert, disguised as Tom Timsbury
Sternum, Rupert's valet
Werewolf *

Chorus and **Dancers** as **Townsfolk**, their **Children,
Birds, Woodland Animals**, etc.

* This character should not be listed in the programme.
See Character and Costume Notes.

MUSICAL NUMBERS

ACT I

1	**Opening Song and Dance**	Gertrude and Chorus
2	**Song**	Rosie and Chorus
3	**Song and Dance**	Principals and Chorus
4	**Comedy Duet and Dance**	Cringe and Cower
5	**"Musical Chairs" Music**	The Band
6	**Comedy Song and Dance**	Grannie, Roxie and Chorus
7	**Romantic Duet**	Rupert and Rosie
8	**Song and March**	Principals and Chorus

ACT II

8a	**Reprise of Song 8**	Principals and Chorus
9	**Dance**	Wildlife
10	**Song and Dance**	Rupert and Wildlife
10a	**Reprise of Song 10**	Wildlife
11	**Comedy Duet and Dance**	Gertrude and Sternum
12	**Song**	Rosie
12a	**Reprise of Song 12**	Rosie
13	**Song and Dance**	Principals and Chorus
14	**Sing-a-long**	Roxie, Reggie and Audience
15	**Finale Song**	All
16	**Finale Song (Reprise)**	All

SYNOPSIS OF SCENES

CHARACTERS AND COSTUMES

Rosie (Principal Girl) is a pretty, petite young woman. She is charm itself, and is never soppy or simpering. It goes without saying that the Prince falls in love with her the moment they meet, and who could blame him. Singing and dancing ability is needed. All her costumes are homespun, but she always looks delightful, even when wearing the dreaded red riding hood. Magnificent Finale costume.

Roxie (Dame) is a well-upholstered, "mutton dressed as lamb" widow. She is raucous, rumbustious and rude, but you can't help liking her. She is on friendly and confidential terms with the audience and never misses an opportunity of involving them. Her make-up, hair and costumes are always outrageous and funny. Apart from her every day outfits, she gets to wear a party frock, a pyjama suit, safari kit, a ludicrous leotard and camouflage costume. Special Finale costume.

Reggie is a dim, but very likeable young buffoon. He instantly makes friends with the audience, especially with the youngsters. He is involved in plenty of audience participation and comic capers. Singing and dancing ability an advantage. Comical costumes including a hunting outfit with breeches wired out to the sides, exercise class gear and camouflage costume. Finale costume.

Grannie Grabbit is a lovable ancient monument. She is strong-willed, independent and likes the odd tipple. She takes a great delight in "putting down" her daughter Roxie. Although bent, wrinkled and short-sighted, she shows amazing agility at times, especially in the party and cottage scenes. This is a character comedienne's part and should be played by an agile actress with "special" dancing ability and a convincing "old age" make-up. Lavender and lace costume with big boots, white wig and steel rimmed spectacles. Glamorous Finale costume.

Gertrude is a buxom country lass who is desperate to find a man before it's too late. She sets her sights on Sternum and uses all her comical "seductive" powers to bag him. A comedienne's part with singing and dancing ability an advantage. Comical "countryfied" costumes. Finale costume.

Count De Cash is an obnoxious aristocrat and self-appointed ruler of the country. He is a posturing dandy with affected manners and speech. He cannot pronounce his Rs. His sneering, supercilious manner should incite the audience into a frenzy of boos and hisses. He wears foppish costumes of the Regency period with tall wigs, make-up and beauty spots. A lace handkerchief and quizzing glass complete his ensemble.

Cringe and **Cower** are the Count's comic footmen. Terrified of losing their jobs—and lives! They carry out their evil master's orders, but they hate him like everyone else and later rebel. A very likeable duo, involved in audience participation and comic antics. Cower is the dimmer of the two. Singing and dancing ability an advantage. They wear ill-fitting footmen's livery and white wigs. Finale costumes.

Prince Rupert (Principal Boy), alias Tom Timsbury, has returned to claim his rightful place on the throne. He is young, dashing and handsome with all the princely qualities and a little something extra—at every full moon he changes into a werewolf! Unaware of this himself, he falls madly in love with Rosie and gives the Count ideas about silver bullets! A strong personality with singing and dancing ability is needed. As to costumes—the actual werewolf is played by a male actor wearing a duplicate of Rupert's costume. Consequently, fishnet tights are definitely out, I'm afraid! Rupert should wear distinctive wide-sleeved blouses and tight-fitting breeches with stockings or thigh boots. Magnificent Finale costume.

Sternum is Rupert's valet. He is the perfect gentleman's gentleman, in the best Jeeves tradition. He is eloquent of speech and dignified in manner. His deadpan expression never alters, except when showing concern for the Prince, and when he finally succumbs to Gertrude's amorous advances. He wears an immaculate morning suit, consisting of a black cut-away coat, black waistcoat, grey pin-striped trousers, wing collar, black tie and black bowler hat.

The Werewolf is Rupert's hairy alter-ego. The part should be played by a male actor for maximum deep growls, snarls and ferocious animal behaviour. He wears a good "full head" werewolf mask with muzzle, fangs and pointed ears, etc. To sustain the belief that it is Rupert who has undergone the transformation, it is important that the actor wears a duplicate of the costume worn by the Prince in the previous scene, i.e. tight-fitting breeches and wide-sleeved blouse. This is ripped open to the waist, revealing a huge, hairy torso. This can be made from "fun fur" attached to a T-shirt. "Wolf paw" gloves and a bushy tail protruding from the seat of his breeches will complete the effect. The werewolf should not be listed in the programme or it will let the cat (or wolf!) out of the bag and spoil the illusion. To receive his well-earned recognition, the werewolf enters for the Finale wearing a large, round "pet-disc" with the actor's name on it. Whether he removes his "head" at this point is left to the discretion of the Director.

The Chorus, **Dancers** and **Children** appears as **Townsfolk**, their **Children**, **Birds** and **Woodland Animals**. All participate in the action and musical numbers.

Paul Reakes

PRODUCTION NOTES

STAGING

Four "full stage" sets are required:
The Town Square—Act I, Scenes 1 and 5
Roxie's Living Room—Act I, Scene 3 and Act II, Scene 3
The Wood—Act II, Scene 1
Grannie's Cottage in the Wood—Act II, Scene 5

These are interlinked by two front-cloths:
The Path Near the Wood—Act I, Scenes 2 and 4, Act II, Scene 4
A Dungeon—Act II, Scene 2

There can be a special Finale setting or the Town Square can be used.

The window in Roxie's room should be fairly large to show off the full moon to good effect.

LIGHTING

It is important that the "full moon" effect is seen clearly through the window on both occasions (Act I, Scene 4 and Act II, Scene 3). In Act II, Scene 1 the transition from night to morning is worth particular attention. In Act II, Scene 5 there is a flash and complete black-out during the action. A good chance for some really "spooky" lighting in certain scenes. If desired, an eerie follow spot can illuminate the werewolf for all his appearances.

EFFECTS

The eerie howling of the werewolf is essential to the action and atmosphere of the panto. It can be a recording, but I strongly advise you to do it live, with a good "howler" using an offstage microphone. Well-controlled ground mist will give certain scenes (Act I, Scene 5 and Act II, Scene 1) a nice "creepy" atmosphere. Recorded music is required for the keep-fit routine involving the audience in Act II. It should be typical of the sort used at exercise classes, and be able to speed up and slow down during the action. A recording of dawn chorus of bird song is required for Act II, Scene 1. The only "flash" occurs in Act II, Scene 5. There is the sound of a heavy door being unlocked etc. in

Act II, Scene 2. This can be a recording or done live. Blanks are fired on (or off) stage in Act I, Scene 5 and Act II, Scene 5. Plaster has to appear to fall from the ceiling in the last of these scenes.

NB: A note in the programme stating that blanks are fired during the show is strongly advisable.

P.R.

Other pantomimes by Paul Reakes published by
Samuel French Ltd:

Babes in the Wood
Dick Turpin
King Arthur,
a pantomime adventure in Camelot
Little Jack Horner
Little Miss Muffet
Old Mother Hubbard
Robinson Crusoe and the Pirates
Santa in Space
Sinbad the Sailor

ACT I

Scene 1

The Town Square of Pantovia. General lighting

Roxie Rumple's house is prominent UR. *Other houses and shops are* L. *Some of them have "For Sale" and "To Let" signs. The backcloth shows the rest of the Square with shops, Town Hall, fountain and the Royal Palace in the distance*

When the Curtain *rises, Gertrude and The Townsfolk are discovered. They go straight into the opening song and dance*

Song 1

First Man All right, everyone! Rosie'll be out in a minute. We'd better have a practice. After three! One—two—three!

Everyone sings "Happy Birthday" to Rosie

Gertrude (*loudly*) Ahhh Meeeen!!

The others laugh

First Man Gertrude! You're not supposed to say "Amen" after "Happy Birthday"!
Gertrude I know that! I jus' like sayin' it, that's all! (*In a sexy voice*) Ahhhh! Meeeen! (*She grabs the First Man*) Give us a kiss, you big hunk!

The others laugh

First Man (*pushing her away*) Ger off! You know I'm walking out with Polly Perkins [or local female]!
Gertrude You've been walking out with *her* for ten years and you don't seem to have covered much ground! (*She sidles up to him. Seductively*) If you walked out with *me* I'd show you a short cut!

Comic business as he fends her off, much to the amusement of the others

First Woman Oh, Gertrude! You're man-mad!

Gertrude (*to the audience*) I am! It's true! I'm desperate to find a boyfriend before I pass my sell-by-date! But this place is 'opeless! No-one 'ere will give me a date!

Little Boy (*moving to her*) I'll give you a date, Gertrude.

Gertrude (*thrilled*) Oh!!

Little Boy 1066! That's a date! (*He laughs*)

Gertrude rounds on him, playfully. The others roar with laughter

Second Man (*very crabbily*) Stop all this nonsense! Stop it! How can you laugh and joke, with Pantovia in the state it's in?!

Gertrude Look out! It's Victor Meldrew!

Second Man Our country has gone to the dogs! Since the Old King died a year ago and that villain Count De Cash appointed himself as Ruler, we've been taxed beyond endurance! Most of the shops have gone out of business! The factories have been forced to close down! People are selling up and moving out! Pantovia is a disgrace!

Gertrude It could be worse! We could be livin' in [local place]!

The others laugh

First Woman If only Prince Rupert would return and take his rightful place on the throne.

Second Man Pah! You can forget that dream! The Prince left here two years ago after a quarrel with his father. He's not been seen or heard of since! You have to face it! Prince Rupert has washed his hands of Pantovia for ever! It's no use looking to him for help!

The others murmur sadly and shake their heads

Gertrude Oh, come on, you pack of miseries! I know livin' 'ere is about as much fun as listenin' to [politician], but we came 'ere to wish Rosie a happy birthday, didn't we?

Others (*brightening*) Yes ... yes...

Gertrude Well, then! Let's forget our troubles and try to be cheerful!

Others Yes!

First Woman Listen! I think I hear her coming out!

Gertrude Right, then! After three! One—two—three!

Everyone starts to sing "Happy Birthday" then breaks off as——

Roxie Rumple enters from her house

The others groan

Roxie Crikey! What it is to be popular! Mornin' all!
Others Mornin', Roxie!
Roxie (*spotting the audience*) Oo! Look! We've got visitors! (*She comes forward and greets the audience*) Hallo, folks!

A few replies

Cor! Is there anybody out there?! Let's join 'ands and try to contact the livin'! I said— (*She yells*) *Hallo!!*

They shout back

That's more like it! Well, what do you think of it so far?

"Rubbish" from the audience

You've got good taste, I'll say that for ya! I'm Roxie Rumple and I live in that semi-skimmed mansion with me daughter Rosie and son Reggie. We're very very poor. (*She sighs and gets them to join in*). Aahh! I'm a widow. (*She sighs again*) Aahh! But my children are a great comfort to me. Oh, I know what you're thinkin'. You don't think I look old enough to be a mummy, do ya?

Slight pause

All right, all right! There's no need to take a vote on it! (*To someone*) You're as young as the man you feel, isn't that right, dear? (*To someone else*) I'm not in bad shape for me age, am I, love? I've got what is known as an hour-glass figure—shame all the sand's gone to the bottom! D'you know, the other day someone said I looked like one of the Spice Girls! Which one? You're dead right—*Old Spice!*
Gertrude (*coming down to her*) Mornin', Roxie!
Roxie 'Ello, Gertrude. And 'ow's Pantovia's answer to [current sex symbol] this mornin'? Any luck findin' the man of your dreams?
Gertrude (*glumly*) Not even a nightmare!
Roxie Well, never mind, dear! Don't give up. You know the old sayin'— "You can lead a horse to water but you can't teach an old dog to lay all its eggs in one basket"! (*To the Townsfolk*) What are you rejects from *Blind Date* doin' 'ere?
First Man We've come to wish Rosie a happy birthday. Where is she?
Roxie I'm keepin' 'er out of the way until our Reggie gets back from the shops.

Gertrude Why?

Roxie I cried meself to sleep last night because I couldn't afford to buy Rosie
    a birthday present. Then, first thing this mornin', I found a five pound note
    down the back of the sofa! I've sent Reggie off to buy 'er a present with
    it. I don't want 'er seein' it before I've wrapped it up, do I?

Gertrude Roxie, that's super!

The others agree

Roxie Well, I only 'ope I've done the right thing! Our Reggie was at the back
    of the queue when they dished out brains!

*Reggie Rumple enters at the back of the Hall. He carries something in a
large paper bag*

Reggie (*calling to the stage*) Yoo hoo!! Hey, Mum! It's me—Reggie!

Roxie Look out! 'Ere comes Mastermind now!

*Reggie makes his way towards the stage through the audience. Comic
business and ad lib as he shakes hands and greets various people on route*

(*After a while, calling to him*) Oy! Who do you think you are—Rikki
    Lake?! Come 'ere!

*Reggie ignores her and continues to chat to the audience. He sits on one
female's knee*

Reggie Rumple, you come 'ere at once! Oh, 'e's awful! 'E'll talk to
    anyone! Leave that woman alone, you don't know where she's been!
    Come 'ere this minute! (*She goes down into the hall and grabs Reggie by
    the ear*)

He yells and squirms as she drags him on to the stage

Reggie Aooow!! Me ear'ole!! Get off!! Le' go!! Aooow!!

Roxie How many times 'ave I told you not to talk to strange people?!

Reggie (*pointing someone out*) But it was [person's name]!

Roxie That's what I mean!

Reggie I think she fancies me! She said I reminded 'er of Leonardo Di
    Caprio.

Roxie Sure she didn't mean Leonardo da Vinci?

Reggie Hey, Mum! Did you hear about the burglar who fell into a cement
    mixer. Now he's a *hardened* criminal! (*He guffaws*)

Roxie (*to the audience*) An' that's what you get for sendin' 'em to [local school]!

Reggie Hey, Mum! I see they're back together again!

Roxie (*all ears*) Who?

Reggie The cheeks of your bum! (*He guffaws*)

She clips him around the ear

Roxie Any more of your nonsense and I'll cut off yer privileges! Now, 'ave you bought our Rosie's birthday present?

Reggie Yeah! An' she's gonna be over the moon with it!

Roxie (*eagerly*) What did you get?

Reggie (*proudly*) It's a signed photograph of a very well known personality!

Roxie and the others "Ooh!" and "Ahh!"

And—he's in—*the nude!*

Even louder reaction

Gertrude (*thrilled*) Cor! Who is it? Robbie Williams?

Reggie Nope!

Woman Brad Pitt?

Reggie Nope!

Roxie Ian Duncan Smith?

Others (*to Roxie, aghast*) Eh?!!

Roxie (*a bit huffily*) Well—each to his own! (*To Reggie*) Oh, stop messin' about and show us!

Others Yes! Let's see it! Come on! (*Etc.*)

Reggie opens the paper bag and takes out a large frame. He holds it up for everyone to see. It is completely blank. It has a backing of thin white paper. The others react

Gertrude But it's blank! There's nothing there!

Reggie Course not! What d'you expect! (*Proudly*) It's a photograph of the invisible man!

The others groan. With icy calm, Roxie moves to Reggie, who is still feeling very pleased with himself

Roxie So! (*She takes the frame*) This is Rosie's birthday present, is it?

Reggie Yeah! The man who sold it to me said I was gettin' a real bargain!

Roxie And that's not all you'll be gettin'! (*She smashes the frame down over his head so that it hangs like a collar around his neck*)

The others roar with laughter

Reggie Help! I've been framed!
Roxie You dozy dunderhead! You no-good nitwit! You've been diddled! Swindled! Cheated out of my last fiver! Ooo! I'll knock you into the middle of next week! (*She violently shakes the frame, causing Reggie to be thrown about*)

Uproar and laughter from the Townsfolk

Rosie Rumple enters from the house. She is puzzled at what is going on

Rosie (*just audibly*) Morning, everyone.
Gertrude (*seeing her*) Mornin', Rosie! (*Yelling to the others*) Oy!!

They all go silent. Roxie stops shaking Reggie. Gertrude points to Rosie

All Happy Birthday, Rosie!
Rosie Thank you all very much.
All (*very sweetly*) Don't mention it.

Uproar breaks out again as Roxie resumes shaking Reggie about

Rosie (*moving over to them*) Mum! Mum! What on earth are you doing to Reggie?
Roxie I gave 'im five pounds to buy you a nice present and 'e comes back with this! (*She pulls the frame from Reggie*)
Rosie (*looking at the frame, stumped for words*) Well … it's … it's very nice. Thank you, Reggie.
Roxie Oh, don't thank 'im! The gormless lump was conned! Some swindlers told 'im it was a photo of the invisible man!
Rosie (*amused*) Oh, Reggie!
Roxie (*to Reggie*) You're two steps from an idiot!
Reggie I'll move, then. (*He does so*) I … I … I'm sorry, Rosie.
Rosie (*going to him*) Oh, that's all right. After all, it's the thought that counts.
Reggie I wish I'd bought you the other thing now.
Rosie What was that?
Reggie Oh, it was ever so good! A huge great bottle of scotch mist!

The Townsfolk laugh

Roxie See! 'E's as daft as a brush!
Reggie Talkin' of brushes. Why do witches ride broomsticks?
Others We don't know. Why *do* witches ride broomsticks?
Reggie So they can *sweep* across the skies! (*He guffaws*)
Roxie *You!!*

Reggie yells and runs into the house, hotly pursued by Roxie

Gertrude (*sadly*) We're sorry we can't afford to buy you a present, Rosie.

Murmurs of agreement from the others

Rosie Times are very hard for all of us. I didn't expect any presents this year.
You all remembered my birthday, that's the main thing. And who needs
presents when you've got true friends.
Gertrude I wish I 'ad a friend. A friend about six foot tall with curly black
hair, heavenly eyes, and... (*getting worked up*) ...and big, bulgin' biceps!
Cor!

The others laugh

First Woman She's off again!
Gertrude (*sulking*) It's not fair!
Rosie (*going to Gertrude*) Don't worry, Gertrude. (*Confidentially*) I haven't
got a boyfriend either.
Gertrude That's only because you 'aven't put yerself on the market yet. I've
'ad the "For Sale" sign up for years!
Rosie Cheer up. I'm sure there's a Mr Right somewhere out there for both
of us.

Song 2

*After the song, Cringe and Cower, the two Footmen, enter DL. They move
LC, stand side by side at attention, facing front*

Gertrude moves over to inspect them

Gertrude (*to Rosie*) 'Ere! I 'ope *these* aren't the Mr Rights you wos on
about! They look more like Mr Leftovers to me!

Roxie and Reggie enter from the house

Roxie What's goin' on now ... (*She sees the Footmen*) Oh, look! It's Wallace
and Gromit!

Reggie That's Cringe and Cower. They're Count De Cash's footmen.

Cringe & Cower Make way! Make way!

Cringe (*announcing*) Make way for his odious obnoxiousness.

Cower His slippery sliminess …

Cringe His creepy crawliness …

Cower His diabolical dastardliness …

Cringe & Cower His awful atrociousness—Count De Cash—Supreme Ruler of Pantovia! (*They do a fanfare*) Ta Raa!

The Townsfolk boo and hiss as the obnoxious, foppish Count De Cash struts on from DL. *He carries a lace handkerchief and a quizzing glass*

Roxie and Reggie encourage the audience to join in with the booing and hissing

Count (*mockingly*) Gweetings! Gweetings! How nice it is to be appweciated! (*To the audience, sneering*) Even by pathetic wiff waff like you! Egad! There's a ghastly smell awound here! (*He puts his handkerchief to his nose*)

Roxie (*moving* C) You're wight! I noticed it the moment you walked in. Pooh!

Count (*moving over and peering at her through his quizzing glass*) Are you addwessing me, you old cwone?

Roxie 'Ere! It's *Mrs* Cwone to you! (*She indicates the glass*) Are you gonna blow bubbles through that in a minute?

Count Don't bandy words with me!

Roxie Why not? They'll match yer bandy legs!

Count (*outraged*) Zounds! This is insuffwable! Don't you know who I am! (*He strikes a foppish pose*)

Roxie No, but I know what you *look* like!

Count (*outraged*) What!!

Rosie (*taking Roxie aside, concerned*) Mum! Be careful!

Roxie Ha! I'm not scared of that piece of puff pastry!

Reggie Nor me! I'm gonna give 'im a piece of my mind! (*He starts to move*)

Roxie (*pushing him back*) No, you're not! You can't spare it! Leave this to Mummy. (*She saunters over the the Count*) What'll 'appen when Prince Rupert returns, eh? You'll be out on yer 'igh falutin' ear'ole then!

Count (*to all, mockingly*) Oh, you poor deluded wiff waff. Do you honestly believe your pwecious Pwince is coming back? He's been gone for two long years! He obviously cares nothing for Pantovia or any of you wabble. He may even be dead! (*Aside to the audience*) And I sincerely hope he is! (*Aloud*) No, I wule Pantovia and I intend to do so for a vewy long time! (*To Roxie*) And as for you, you diswespectful old dish wag— (*To Cringe and Cower*) Men! Seize that woman!

*Cringe and Cower move over and take hold of Roxie. She struggles in vain.
Reaction from the others*

Six months in my deepest dungeon will teach her to have some wespect!

Uproar from the others

Roxie You can't do that! I'm allergic to dungeons! I've got an allegory!
Rosie (*rushing to the Count*) Please... You can't do this!
Count (*peering at her through his glass and obviously liking what he sees*)
Mmm! And who are you, pway?
Rosie I am Rosie Rumple. Her daughter. Oh, please don't put her in prison.
Today is my birthday and t'would break my poor old mother's heart to be
parted from us. Oh, please have mercy! (*Quick aside to Roxie*) Cry, Mum,
cry!
Roxie (*playing it up for all it's worth*) Boo hoo! Waaaah!!

Reggie falls to his knees and wrings his hands

Reggie Don't take my Mummy away! Waaaah!!

Reggie and Roxie make an awful noise between them

Count Egad! Desist at once!

They go silent

(*To Rosie*) Vewy well, M'dear. (*Smarmily*) As you are such a delightful
little cweature and today is your birthday, I will let it pass. (*To Cringe and
Cower*) Welease the baggage!

Cringe and Cower let go of Roxie

(*To Roxie*) But be warned! Any further displays of diswespect and it's the
dungeon—or worse! (*To the others*) That applies to all of you! (*To the
audience*) Even you!!

By-play with the audience

(*To all*) I will take my leave of you now. (*He turns to the exit* DL)
Roxie (*aside*) Hip hurray!
Count (*spinning round*) What was that?!
Roxie (*beaming and waving*) Have a nice day!

Count (*with a flick of his hanky*) Pah! Wetched peasants!

The Count struts off DL, *followed by Cringe and Cower*

Reggie mimics the Count's walk and manner, then blows a loud raspberry after him. The others laugh

Reggie Hey! I've just 'ad a thought!

Roxie Well, look after it, 'cos it's on strange ground.

Reggie Rosie's gonna get a present today after all! You've forgotten Grannie! She *always* brings Rosie a present on 'er birthday!

Roxie (*enthused*) Oh, yes! Grannie Grabbit's prezzy! There you are, Rosie! There's somethin' to look forward to!

Rosie (*with no enthusiasm*) Yes.

Roxie Well, don't sound so enthusimastic!

Rosie But I know exactly what it'll be. *Another* red riding hood! She's given me one every birthday since I was two years old. The novelty's worn off a bit.

Roxie (*to the audience*) Flippin' ungrateful kids! Who'd 'ave 'em! (*To Rosie*) Look, just pretend to like it, for yer Gran's sake, eh?

Rosie (*sighing*) I'll try.

Roxie You don't want to hurt 'er feelings, do ya? I know she's a cantankerous old biddy, but 'er heart's in the right place—even if 'er teeth sometimes aren't!

Reggie (*looking off* L) Here comes Grannie now!

Old Grannie Grabbit hobbles on DL. *She carries a parcel*

Grannie Mornin', all!

All Mornin', Grannie!

Roxie (*going to Grannie*) Hallo, dear.

Grannie (*peering at her*) Who are you?

Roxie I'm Roxie! Yer daughter!

Grannie Thank goodness for that! Lummy! I thought they'd moved the Millennium Dome! You're puttin' on weight, girl!

Roxie Oh, it's just middle-age spread!

Grannie Well, stop eatin' it, then! (*She cackles*) Now, where's the birthday girl? Where's my little Rosie?

Rosie Here I am, Grannie.

Grannie hobbles over to Rosie and kisses her

Grannie 'Appy birthday, lovie. 'Ere! Tell yer mother to stop usin' so much make-up. I've seen less paint on a double-decker bus!

Roxie Cheeky old biddy!

Grannie (*rounding on Roxie and waving her stick*) I 'eard that! Watch it!

The others laugh

(*Going back to Rosie*) Well, 'ere you are, Rosie love. Many 'appy returns of the day! (*She hands Rosie the parcel*)

Rosie Thanks, Grannie. (*Doing her best*) I ... I wonder what it can be. (*She opens the parcel and hands the wrapping to Reggie. She holds up the dreaded red riding hood. Still doing her best*) A red riding hood! Thank you, Grannie. It's ... it's lovely.

Roxie (*threateningly*) *Just* what you wanted, isn't it?

Rosie Oh, yes! Just what I wanted.

Grannie (*proudly*) Made it all meself! Every stitch! Took me 'ours and 'ours! I'm dyin' to see 'ow well it fits, but after walkin' all that way from my cottage in the wood, I'm in need of some refreshment. (*To Roxie, very pointedly*) It's a very *long*, *arduous* and *exhaustin'* trip for someone of my age. Not that I'm complainin'.

Roxie (*aside*) Oh, she does prattle on!

Grannie Eh?!

Roxie I said—I'll put the kettle on.

Grannie Oh, that'll go down a treat! A nice cuppa tea— (*she nudges Roxie*) wi' a drop of somethin' in it. No milk, no sugar and not too much tea— come to think of it—leave the tea out altogether!

Grannie hobbles off into Roxie's house. Reggie follows

Gertrude and the Townsfolk exit

Rosie is looking forlornly at the riding hood

Roxie Well, don't stand there lookin' at it, put it on!

Rosie Oh, Mum! Do I have to?

Roxie Yes! Yer Gran'll only 'ang about 'ere until you do! And I've only got four bottles of gin left. Put it on—*now*!

Roxie exits into the house

Rosie (*to the audience*) Oh, dear! (*She shows off the riding hood*) What do you think? It's hardly [well-known fashion designer], is it? Oh, well, I suppose I'd better put it on. I don't want to hurt dear old Gran's feelings. (*Confidentially*) I'll hide it in the back of the wardrobe with all the others as soon as she's gone home. (*She puts on the riding hood*)

As she is doing so, Count De Cash enters UL

Unseen by Rosie, he stands watching her through his quizzing glass

(*To the audience*) There! How does it look? (*She does a twirl and is startled to see the Count watching her*)

Count (*with a mocking laugh*) Haw! Haw! It makes you look like a letter box! The kindest thing to do would be to have it destwoyed immediately!

Rosie (*in spite of herself*) Well, I think it's very nice! It's a birthday present from my grandmother, and I don't care what *you* think! (*She turns away from him*)

Count (*to the audience*) She's a vewy appetising little cwacker, but sadly without any taste! (*To Rosie*) M'dear! You call that disgusting wag a birthday pwesent! These are what I call birthday pwesents! (*He calls*) Men!

Cringe and Cower enter UL. *They are practically hidden behind two enormous gift-wrapped boxes*

As soon as I learned it was your birthday I purchased them for you. And they're not from [local shop] either!

Rosie No, thank you. I never accept gifts from strange men! (*She moves* DR)

Cringe (*to the audience, from around the side of his box*). Sensible girl!

Cower (*to the audience, from around his box*). And they don't come much stranger than 'im!

Count (*smarming up to Rosie*) M'dear, I would like you to accompany me back to the Palace.

Cringe & Cower (*to the audience*) Ha! Ha!

Count I have awanged a little birthday party. Just for the two of us.

Cringe & Cower (*to the audience*) Ho! Ho!

Count And in the evening I will show you my artefacts.

Cringe & Cower (*to the audience*) Way! Hay!

Rosie (*stiffly*) Thank you for the offer, but I shall be spending my birthday with my family.

Count (*scoffing*) Your family! Pah! That collection of common clodhoppers! I can offer you expensive wine—sumptuous food—exquisite suwoundings.

Cringe (*to Cower, around the box*) 'E can't be takin' 'er to [local pub or restaurant] then!

Cower (*to Cringe, around the box*) No! Sounds more like [local chip shop or transport café] to me!

Count I am afwaid you have no choice in the matter, m'dear. As your wuler, I *command* you to accompany me! (*He grabs her by the wrist*)

Rosie (*struggling*) Let go of me!!

Cower We've got to do somethin' to 'elp that poor girl!
Cringe Follow me!

Cringe and Cower rush across and get between Rosie and the Count. A slapstick routine follows in which they use their boxes to prevent the Count getting near Rosie. Comic business as they bump into him, crush him between the boxes and trip him up, etc. At one point the Count falls to the ground and they put one of the boxes (with a false bottom) completely over him. He crawls about with it on his back. Rosie, the silly girl, remains to laugh at the spectacle. Eventually, the Count disentangles himself from the box and roars at Cringe and Cower

  Cringe and Cower run out, taking the boxes with them

Count (*advancing on Rosie, with a lecherous chuckle*) Hee! Hee! Hee!
  Come here, m'dear!

He pursues Rosie around the stage. He finally grabs her by the wrist and drags her to the exit DL. They struggle

Rosie Let go! *Help!* Leave me alone! *Help!*

  Handsome Prince Rupert enters at the back. He is followed by Sternum, a very dignified-looking man wearing a morning suit and bowler hat. They take stock of the situation and move DC

Rupert I say! Unhand that young woman at once!

The Count continues to struggle with Rosie

  Roxie, Grannie and Reggie rush from the house

  Gertrude and the Townsfolk rush on

  Cringe and Cower enter

Roxie What's goin' on?!
Grannie Oy! What's 'e doin' to our Rosie?
Rupert (*to the Count*) I would strongly advise you to leave that young
  woman alone, sir!
Count (*still holding Rosie*) And what if I won't?!
Rupert Then I shall be forced to knock you down.

Reaction from all the others

Count You insolent young puppy! Do you know who I am?!
Rupert An ill-mannered oaf by the look of it.

Delighted reaction from the others

Count I am Count De Cash! The wuler of Pantovia! Who are you, upstart?

Sternum clears his throat and is about to speak, but Rupert quickly stops him

Rupert It doesn't matter who *I* am. Now, for the last time, will you unhand
that young woman?
Count I will not!
Rupert Very well! (*He goes over and socks the Count on the jaw, knocking
him to the ground*)
Others (*cheering*) Hurray!!

*The Count sits up, nursing his jaw. His wig is over one eye. The others roar
with laughter. Livid with rage, the Count staggers to his feet and adjusts his
wig*

Count (*to Rupert*) You will pay dearly for this outwage! (*To Cringe and
Cower*) Seize that man! *Seize him!*

*Cringe and Cower move towards Rupert, but Sternum quickly steps in front
of them. Everyone watches in mute wonderment. With a completely deadpan
expression, Sternum carefully removes his bowler and hands it to Rupert with
a bow. He turns back to the dumbstruck Cringe and Cower. He bows to them,
then adopts the Queensbery boxing stance. They back away as he advances
on them with a jabbing fist*

Cringe and Cower yell and run out

*The others clap. Sternum bows, retrieves his bowler and carefully puts it back
on*

You've not heard the last of this! (*To the audience*) Any of you!

*Amid jeers and boos from the others and the audience, the Count tries to
make a dignified exit* DL, *but the effects of his recent blow make it a rather
wobbly departure*

Everyone moves in to congratulate Rupert

Grannie (*shaking his hand*) Right on! Nice one, young man! Cor! You gave 'im a right belter! (*She demonstrates*) Zap!! Kerpow!! Wallop!! (*In her exuberance she almost falls over*)

Rosie (*to Rupert, a little shyly*) Thank you very much for coming to my assistance.

Rupert It was a pleasure, Miss ... er ...

Rosie (*offering her hand*) My name's Rosie. Rosie Rumple.

Rupert (*taking her hand*) Very pleased to meet you, Rosie. Very pleased indeed.

Pause as they gaze into each other's eyes

Roxie (*with an extra loud cough*) Ahhem!!

Rosie (*coming down to earth*) Oh, yes! Let me introduce my family. My mother. My grandmother. And my brother, Reggie.

Gertrude pushes in with her hand held out, eager to be introduced

Oh, and this is my friend, Gertrude.

Rupert How do you do, Gertrude. (*He takes her hand*)

Gertrude (*pulling him up close and fluttering her eyelashes at him*) Very well, thank you, how do *you*! You can call me Gert an' leave the *rude* bit out! (*She does a soppy giggle*)

Rupert has difficulty extracting his hand from Gertrude's grasp

Grannie And what's *your* name, young man?

Sternum clears his throat and is about to speak, but Rupert cuts in quickly

Rupert My name is Tom. Tom ... er ... Tom Timsbury. And this is my manservant, Sternum.

Sternum (*addressing the gathering in his dulcet tones*) It gives me monumental gratification to be in close proximity with such a convivial populace. (*He bows*)

Others (*agog*) Eh?!!

Rupert (*with a laugh*) That means—he's pleased to meet you all.

Roxie Good! I thought 'e'd swallowed the dictionary!

Rupert Oh, Sternum always uses more words than are necessary.

Gertrude (*sidling up to Sternum and fluttering her eyelashes at him*) You'd only 'ave to say *one* word to me!

Sternum (*raising an eyebrow*) Yes?

Gertrude *That's* the word!

Rupert (*to Rosie*) I'm on a walking holiday and have only just arrived in your

country. Tell me, that scoundrel who was pestering you, is he really the
Ruler of Pantovia?

Rosie Yes, unfortunately.

Second Man And he's bleeding us dry with his confounded taxes!

*Angry murmurs of agreement from the others. Rupert and Sternum quickly
exchange glances*

Rupert (*to Rosie*) That ... that sounds awful.

Grannie It is! None of us 'ave got two 'a'p'nnies to scratch our——

Roxie (*warningly*) *Mum!!*

Grannie —noses with!

Reggie (*to Rupert*) It's our Rosie's birthday today and we can't even afford
to give 'er a party.

Rupert Many happy returns.

Rosie Thank you.

Rupert No birthday party, eh! That'll never do. I would be honoured if you'd
allow me to pay for one.

Rosie But...

Rupert Sternum!

Sternum Yes, sir?

Rupert Have you got the groats?

Reggie No, I think 'e always stands like that! (*He guffaws*)

*Roxie clips Reggie around the ear. Sternum, closely followed by Gertrude,
moves down to Rupert. As if by magic, he produces a salver with a money bag
on it. With a bow he holds it out to Rupert*

Rupert (*taking the bag*) This should be enough to provide a splendid party
for all your family and friends. (*He holds the bag out to Rosie*)

Rosie (*overwhelmed*) I ... I don't know what to say!

Roxie (*aside to Rosie*) I do! Take the money!

Rosie Thank you very much, Tom. (*She reaches for the bag*)

Rupert (*withdrawing it*) There is a condition, however—I get an invitation.

Rosie Of course you do! You shall be my guest of honour! (*She takes the bag*)

Grannie (*kicking up her heels*) Whoopee!! There's gonna be a party!

Song 3

*This should be a lively song and dance for everyone. Comic antics from
Grannie, Roxie and Reggie. Gertrude plays up to the dignified Sternum. A
tableau finish on the last note of music, and the Lights fade to Black-out*

Music to cover the scene change

A Path Near the Wood

Tabs or front-cloth showing trees and undergrowth. General lighting

Cringe creeps on from DR

He looks about to make sure the coast is clear, then calls off R *in a "stage whisper"*

Cringe It's all right. 'E's not 'ere.
Cower (*off* R, *in "stage whisper"*) Are you sure?
Cringe (*in "stage whisper"*) Of course I'm sure!
Cower (*in "stage whisper"*) Why are you whisperin', then?
Cringe (*in "stage whisper"*) I'm not... (*bellowing*) whisperin'!! Come 'ere!

Cower creeps on from DR, *very scared*

Cower H-How d'you know 'e's not h-hidin' somewhere! Waitin' to p-pounce on us!
Cringe I 'adn't thought of that! Let's ask the spectators. (*He indicates the audience*)
Cower Hey, that's a bit rude!
Cringe What is?
Cower Callin' 'em speckled taters! (*He peers out*) They look more like cauliflowers to me! Except *that* one over there! (*He points to someone*) 'E's definitely a brussels sprout!
Cringe (*to the audience*) Take no notice. 'E used to live at [local place]! Now, have you seen our boss? Count De Cash. Y'know the one with the funny walk!

They mimic the Count's walk and manner

'Ave you seen 'im? No? Good! We're keepin' out of 'is way. 'E's been in a fouler mood than usual ever since that young chap thumped 'im this mornin'!
Cower Cor! That was good! Wack! I'd love to 'ave done that! Only twice as 'ard! Smack!
Cringe Same 'ere! We 'ate 'im as well, y'see. We'd leave tomorrow, but jobs are very 'ard to find, aren't they?
Cower Yeah, so are [topical gag]!
Cringe The trouble is, workin' for 'im, we don't 'ave any friends! (*He sighs*) Aah!

They encourage the audience to "aah" with them

Cower You'll be our friends, won't you, folks?

"Yes" from the audience

Cringe Great! Just think, all those nice people out there are our friends.
Cower Yeah! (*He puts his arm around Cringe*) And we've still got each other!
Cringe Don't spoil it!

Song 4

A comedy duet. Perhaps Cole Porter's Friendship, *or something that involves the audience*

Now that you're our mates we wanna share our sweets with you.

They take out bags of sweets

Cower We swiped 'em from old fancy pants! They're 'is favourite ones too!
Cringe 'E's got boxes full! 'E won't miss these!

They throw the sweets out to the audience, ad lib

Count De Cash enters from DL, *and moves behind them*

The audience will start shouting "He's behind you!", etc.

What? Behind us? Is there someone behind us?
Cower Is it our boss? Is it old fancy pants?

"Yes!" from the audience

Cringe (*to Cower*) They're 'avin' us on! 'E's not really there! (*To the audience*) Is 'e?

"Yes!" from the audience

Cower Oh, no, he isn't!

Routine with the audience

Cringe (*to Cower*) Let's look!

Business with them turning around and the Count always keeping behind them. This is repeated ad lib. Finally, they come face to face with the Count and react

Cower (*timidly holding out his sweet bag*) W-would you like a sweetie?
Count (*looking in the bag*) They look wemarkably like my favouwites. (*Exploding*) They are mine!!

Cringe and Cower yell and run out

(*To the audience*) Have those two blockheads been giving you *my* sweets! How dare they! Give them back at once!

He may get pelted with sweets!

On second thoughts, don't bother! I can't eat sweets at the moment. My mouth is still too sore from where that young vawlet stwuck me! (*He delicately touches his lip*). Egad! I can't imagine what damage he's done to my lip gloss! (*Increasingly venomous*) But I shall get my wevenge on him! Oh, yes! No-one widicules Count De Cash and gets away with it! No-one!

By-play with the audience, then he looks off R

Ah! Here comes the young dog now! I will hide, and may overhear something to speed my wevenge!

Amid boos, the Count exits DL

Rupert enters DR, followed by Sternum. The young Prince is on cloud nine

Rupert (*rapturously repeating the name*) Rosie! Rosie! Oh, don't you think it's a beautiful name, Sternum? (*Ecstatically*) Rosie!
Sternum It has a certain resonance that is acoustically acceptable to the ossicles of the ear.
Rupert (*not really understanding a word*) Quite! But what about the girl herself! What do you think of *her*? (*Quickly*) And in *one* word, please, Sternum.

Sternum thinks for a second

Sternum Pulchritudinous.
Rupert (*not having a clue what it means*) Er... Exactly! I must confess, Sternum. I have fallen hopelessly in love with Rosie Rumple.

Sternum But, Your Highness…

Rupert Shh! Keep your voice down. I don't want anyone to know I'm Prince Rupert yet.

Sternum But I understood it was Your Highness's intention to resume your rightful place on the throne of Pantovia.

Rupert And I still intend to do so! Especially after discovering that a villain like this De Cash has taken over! But before I make my true identity known I want to find out what Rosie's feelings are towards me. At the party tonight I intend to declare my love for her as common Tom Timsbury. If she reciprocates, I'll know she loves me for myself and not because of who I am.

Sternum I stand in admiration of Your Highness's integrity and please accept my felicitations on the young lady, but … there is a matter of extreme urgency which I must acquaint Your Highness with.

Rupert Will it take long?

Sternum I shall endeavour to be as economical with the information as true clarification of the facts will allow, Your Highness.

Rupert (*smiling*) You're already off to a bad start, Sternum! Just give me the edited highlights.

Sternum (*clearing his throat and preparing for a startling announcement*) Your Highness, it grieves me to have to inform you that——

Suddenly, Rosie and Gertrude enter DR. *They carry empty baskets*

Rosie & Gertrude Hallo!!

Rupert immediately turns his attention to Rosie

Rupert (*going to Rosie*) Hallo, Rosie.
Rosie Hallo, Tom.

They gaze at each other. Gertrude moves over to Sternum and stands very close, gazing up at him with a big soppy grin

Gertrude Hallo, Mr Sternum!
Sternum (*preoccupied and hardly noticing her*) Good afternoon, Miss.

Gertrude is deflated

Rosie Gertrude and I are just going to the shops to buy food for the party tonight.
Rupert Splendid! We'll come along and help. Let me take your basket.
Rosie Thank you, Tom.

They gaze adoringly at each other again. Without breaking the gaze, Rosie hands Rupert her basket. He takes it and immediately holds it out to Sternum's direction. With a pained look, Sternum takes the basket. The lovers continue to gaze at each other. Comic business with Gertrude holding out her basket to Sternum. He ignores her and moves to Rupert. He gives his polite cough

Rupert (*coming down to earth*) Eh? Oh, what is it, Sternum?
Sternum (*in hushed tones*) Your Highness, I must inform you that——
Rupert (*dismissing him*) Later, Sternum, later. We've got shopping to do. (*He turns back to Rosie and offers her his arm*)

Rosie takes Rupert's arm and they drift out DR, *still gazing at each other*

Comic business as Gertrude coyly offers her arm to Sternum. He takes no notice and walks to exit DR. *She trots after him with her arm held out*

Sternum exits

Gertrude drops her arm and shrugs

Gertrude (*to the audience*) Well, girls, if at first you don't succeed! Oh, Mr Sternum! Wait for me!

Gertrude runs out DR

Count De Cash creeps on DL

Count (*to the audience*) So! That young upstart is weally Pwince Wupert, eh! And he's come back to claim the thwone! This could mean the end of my days as Wuler of Pantovia! No more wealth! No more power! It's not fair!! (*He has a tantrum and stamps his feet, then is struck by a thought*) But wait! No-one knows who he is yet! The lovesick fool wishes to keep his identity a secwet until the party tonight! (*Cunningly*) What if he were to disappear before then! No-one would be any the wiser, and I can cawwy on wuling the countwy! (*With devilish glee*) Oh, yes! All I have to do is think of some way of getting wid of him! But fear not, I will think of something because I'm vewy clever that way! Oh, yes, I am!

By-play with the audience

Amid boos and hisses the Count exits DL, *as the Lights fade to Black-out*

Music to cover the scene change

SCENE 3

Rosie's Birthday Party

Side wings and back wall represent the living-room of Roxie's house. In the back wall C *is a large window through which the full moon can later be seen. Entrances* R *and* L. *The room is festooned with trimmings and balloons. Above the window hangs a "Happy Birthday Rosie" banner. General lighting*

The party is in full swing and very noisy. Everyone is wearing party hats. The Townsfolk fill the back, watching a riotous game of musical chairs in progress DS. *This involves Roxie (outrageously dressed for the party), Reggie, Grannie, Gertrude and Sternum. The latter looks and feels very out of place. Especially wearing a silly party hat instead of his bowler*

Song 5

This should be a noisy comedy routine with lots of sitting on laps, falling on the floor, etc. Comic by-play with the band will also add to the fun. It ends with Grannie being the winner. All cheer and clap the old lady. Her chair is cleared to the side

Reggie Well done, Gran!
Grannie Oh, there's life in the old gal yet! I've still got plenty of "get up an' go", y'know! (*She attempts a high kick and almost falls over*)
Roxie Yes, but most of it's got up an' left. Why don't you sit down before you blow a gasket.
Grannie Oh, fiddlesticks! Don't be such a party pooper! You'd 'ave a bit more energy if you got rid of some of this excess baggage!
Reggie I'm not sayin' she's fat, but every time she falls over she rocks 'erself to sleep tryin' to get up again!

Reggie and Grannie and the others roar with laughter. Roxie clips Reggie around the ear. The three move L. *Gertrude brings Sternum forward, clinging to his arm*

Gertrude Did you enjoy that game of musical chairs, Mr Sternum?
Sternum (*trying to be polite*) Ecstatically, Miss.
Gertrude The bit I enjoyed most was when I sat on your lap! Did *you* enjoy that bit as well?
Sternum (*doing his best*) It was most uplifting, Miss.
Gertrude (*squirming with delight*) Ooo! You saucy so an' so, you! (*She nudges him and giggles*)

With a pained expression, Sternum disentangles himself from Gertrude and moves over to Roxie, who has her back to him. He does his polite cough

Roxie (*reacting to the audience*) Crikey! Someone's got clutch trouble!

Sternum Excuse me, Madam. I am anxious to ascertain the whereabouts of my Master.

Roxie Oh, 'e's still out in the garden with our Rosie. They've been out there for ages! I can't think what they're doin' all this time!

Grannie Well, they're not plantin' spuds, are they! What d'you *think* they're doin'?

Roxie They can't be lookin' at the flowers. It's too dark!

Reggie They could be waitin' for the *bulbs* to come up! (*He guffaws*)

Roxie raises her hand, but Reggie dives for cover behind Grannie

Grannie (*to Roxie*) Oh, you are thick! They're canoodlin'.

Roxie *Canoein'!!* What in? The bird bath?!

Grannie I said *canoodlin'*! Y'know! 'E's chattin' 'er up!

Roxie *What!!* Oh, I'll soon sort 'im out!

Sternum Do not be alarmed, Madam. My Master is the very essence of probity.

Roxie Yes, it's the *"prob"* bit that worries me!

Grannie Oh, leave 'em alone! Remember what you were like at their age!

Roxie (*after a thought*) That *settles* it! I'm goin' out there! (*She moves to go*)

Grannie (*pulling her back*) Come 'ere! I'm ready for more fun an' larks! Let's give 'em our famous party piece!

Roxie (*groaning*) Oh, no!

Grannie Oh, yes! (*To the others*) You want to see our party piece, don't ya?

Others Yes!

Grannie (*to the audience*) And so do you, don't ya, folks?

"Yes!" from the audience

(*To Roxie*) There!

Roxie Oh... All right, then!

Grannie (*to the band*) Hit it!!

Song 6

A comedy duet for Grannie and Roxie. There should be a "dance break" for them while the chorus take up the singing. Grannie really excels herself— perhaps even doing a cartwheel! It ends with her doing the splits, and Roxie— not! All clap and cheer. Grannie has to be helped up

Rosie and Rupert enter R. *She still wears the red riding hood over her party dress*

Reggie (*seeing him*) Look out! Here comes [current romantic couple in the news or on TV] now!

Roxie (*to them*) An' what, may I ask, 'ave you two been doin' all this time?

Rosie Just walking and talking. It was so quiet and peaceful in the garden. (*Gazing at Rupert*) Wasn't it, Tom?

Rupert (*gazing at her*) It was—enchanting!

Reggie turns to the audience and does "sick-making" actions

Gertrude (*sidling up to Sternum*) Oh, it sounds *heavenly*, doesn't it? (*All soppy*) I'd love to go for a walk in the garden. (*She rests her head on his shoulder and gazes up at him*) Wouldn't *you*, Mr Sternum?

Sternum moves away, causing her to topple sideways. He goes to Rupert

Sternum Excuse me, sir.

Rupert (*without taking his eyes from Rosie*) Go away, Sternum.

Sternum (*a little stung*) Very good, sir.

Grannie (*getting the others' attention*) Well! Night, night, all! It's time I was gettin' back to me cottage.

Rosie But it's late, Grannie. Why don't you stay the night?

Grannie No thanks, lovie. I wouldn't be able to sleep a wink between strange sheets. And I know yer mother doesn't use Lenor!

Rosie But, Grannie ...

Roxie (*taking her aside*) The longer she stays, the longer you've got to wear *that*! (*She points to the red riding hood*)

Rosie True! (*Quickly*) Good-night, then, Gran!

Roxie (*to Gran*) Our Reggie will see you back to yer cottage.

Reggie (*aghast*) Ehh?!! You ... you want me to go into that creepy wood at this time of night! It's all dark an' sc-scary!

Roxie Listen! The scariest thing in that wood *is* yer Gran! Do it!!

Grannie (*to Reggie*) Come on, fearless Fred!

Grannie hobbles out R, *dragging the reluctant Reggie with her. Roxie and the Townsfolk follow them out, with ad lib of "Good-night! Thanks for a smashing party", etc., etc.*

Rosie and Rupert resume gazing at each other. Gertrude sidles up to Sternum. Just as she gets near, he moves away to Rupert

Sternum Excuse me, sir.

Rupert (*coming down to earth*) What?! Oh! Are you still here, Sternum?

Sternum Yes, sir. (*Confidentially*) I still have a matter of grave importance to discuss with you ...

Rupert (*taking him aside in hushed tones*) Not *now*! You know I want to be alone with Rosie. I told you why!

Sternum But, sir...

Rupert (*aloud, indicating Gertrude*) Why don't you see Gertrude home, Sternum.

Gertrude (*thrilled and moving in close to Sternum*) Ooo! Ta ever so muchly, thank you kindly!

Sternum (*persisting*) But, *sir*...

Rupert (*firmly*) That's an order, Sternum!

Sternum (*resigned*) Very good, sir.

Gertrude (*taking his arm and cuddling up*) We'll take the short cut. (*Aside to the audience*) Via Lovers' Lane!

Wearing a pained expression, Sternum is whisked out R *by an ecstatic Gertrude*

Rupert Rosie, did you mean what you said in the garden just now?

Rosie What, about how well our radishes were doing?

Rupert (*with a laugh*) No. About how well we get on with each other. Did you mean it?

Rosie Of course I meant it, Tom.

Rupert Have you... Have you thought that perhaps it might be something more than just "getting on" between us?

Rosie (*a little shyly*) Well—I did hope that you might feel the same way about *me*—as I do about *you*.

Rupert Does that mean... (*Overjoyed, he takes her in his arms*) Oh, Rosie, darling! Of course I feel the same way!

Song 7

A romantic duet with romantic lighting. After the song, the Lighting returns to normal

Now that I know you love me, Rosie, I have something very important to tell you. I am——

Roxie enters R

Roxie Phew!! All that jiggin' about 'as played 'avoc with me pet corns! All I wanna do is put me feet up, an' 'ave a nice cuppa tea! (*She flops on to a* *chair* R) Go and put the kettle on, Rosie. I'm gaggin'! (*She removes a shoe and massages her foot*)

Rosie looks questioningly at Rupert. He nods, and she moves to the exit L. *She stops and they blow kisses*

Rosie exits

Roxie replaces her shoe and looks across at the grinning Rupert

You're lookin' very pleased with yerself, young man.
Rupert (*moving* DL, *ecstatically*) Oh, I am—*I am!*
Roxie (*to the audience*) Crikey! I've never seen anyone get *that* excited over a cuppa tea before!
Rupert Mrs Rumple, I have some news for you. Your daughter—Rosie——
Roxie Yes, I know 'er name.
Rupert We... We love each other!
Roxie (*leaping up, all in one breath*) What!! But, I don't know you! Who are you? 'Ave you got any money? Where do you come from? Where are you goin'? 'Ave you got any money? Who are your parents? 'Ave *they* got any money? Oh, I don't know what to say! I'm speechless! (*She flops back on to the chair*)
Rupert As soon as Rosie returns I have a very important announcement to make.

At this point the full moon is seen clearly through the windows at the back. During Roxie's monologue that follows, unseen by Roxie, Rupert turns and sees the moon. He reacts and becomes strangely affected. He twitches. He pulls at his clothing. He starts scratching. With a convulsion, he drops to the floor on all fours. His tongue hangs out and he starts panting. He gives a low growl and crawls over to where Roxie is sitting. Roxie is completely oblivious of what is happening to Rupert or the audience's response to it

Roxie (*facing front, rambling*) Well, I 'ope you don't think she's got any money! Because we're very poor, y'know. Very poor! Mind you, I'm no stranger to poverty. I've known it all my life! Oh, yes! Up until the age of ten I thought knives and forks were jewellery! My mother used to take the bones out of 'er corset to make soup with! My father didn't earn enough to keep a mouse alive! 'E was a tailor in a nudist camp! And it was just the same when I first got married. We were so poor I 'ad to put two babies in one nappy! It was the only way to make ends meet!

Rupert sniffs her loudly at this point, then bounds out on all fours

I know! It makes ya wanna weep, dunnit! (*She is choked up*) So, if you think we've got any money—you're barkin' up the wrong tree! I... (*She turns and finds she is alone*) Well, I'll be jiggered! 'E's gorn an' gorn!

Rosie enters L

Rosie The tea's nearly ready—where's Tom?
Roxie (*getting up and going to her*) I dunno. It's funny. 'E was 'ere a minute ago. Per'aps 'e's gone to see a man about a dog!

The eerie howling of a wolf is heard, filling the stage and auditorium

And it sounds like 'e's found one!!

Quick Black-out

Sinister horror film type music is played during the scene change

SCENE 4

The Path Near the Wood

As Act I, Scene 2. The lighting is dark and creepy. Full moon effect on front-cloth. The stage is empty

The music fades out. A pause. Howling is heard, then silence. Another pause

Suddenly a ferocious and furry Werewolf leaps from the wings and lands on stage DR. *See Character and Costume Notes*

This should give the audience a fright. The Werewolf prawls up and down, snarling and growling at the audience and lashing out with its claws

The Werewolf turns and howls up at the moon, then, snarling at the audience, it bounds out DL

A slight pause, then Grannie hobbles on from DR. *Reggie follows, very scared and hanging back*

Grannie (*coming* C) Oh, come on lad! You're slower than a snail with bunions! I wanna get to me cottage before *this* Christmas, not *next*!
Reggie (*moving to her*) I-I don't like this place, Grannie! It's sp-spooky! (*He looks about and shivers*) It gives me the wi-willies!

Grannie Oh, fiddlesticks! You're actin' like a big baby! There's nothin' to
be scared of around 'ere!

Howling is heard. Reggie freezes in terror. Grannie takes no notice

Reggie (*trembling*) D-Did you h-hear that?
Grannie What?
Reggie Th-That noise!
Grannie Oh, pardon me! It's probably them pickled onions I 'ad at the party.
Reggie No! It was a h-horrible h-howlin' noise!
Grannie Rubbish! You imagined it!
Reggie I never! (*To the audience*) You 'eard it as well, didn't you, folks?

"Yes!" from the audience

Grannie Oh, you don't want to listen to them! They've probably been down
the [local pub]!

Howling is heard. Reggie yells and clings to Grannie

Reggie Aahhh! There it is again!
Grannie (*smacking his hand*) Oh, be'ave yerself, Reggie! Act yer age! It's
only a bird!
Reggie (*aghast*) A bird!! I'd 'ate to see the sort of bird that makes a noise like
that!

Unseen by them, the Werewolf creeps on from DL, *and prowls about behind
them. The audience will be shouting "It's behind you!", etc.*

(*To the audience, terrified*) I-Is there something behind us?!

"Yes" from the audience

(*To Grannie*) Th-Th-There's something behind us, Gran!!
Grannie Oh, stuff an' nonsense! They're playin' tricks on you! (*To the
audience*) Now then, we're gonna 'ave a look, and woe betide you lot if
there's nothin' there! (*She propels Reggie around*)

*Comic business with them turning and the Werewolf always keeping behind
them. This is repeated a couple of times. They face front again. Reggie,
shaking with fear, covers his eyes*

(*To the audience*) Oh, I've 'ad enough of 'is messin' about! I'll see meself
'ome! Night, all!

Grannie hobbles out DL

The Werewolf takes Grannie's place beside Reggie. It gives him a sniff

Reggie (*thinking she is still there*) Oh, Grannie, I'm s-so s-scared! I don't know what I'd do if you weren't with me! (*He uncovers his eyes, but keeps them tightly shut*) I wouldn't be so frightened if I could hold your hand. (*Whining*) Oh, please let me hold your hand, Grannie! (*He reaches down and takes the Werewolf's paw*)

The Werewolf gives a puzzled growl

Oh, that's better. I don't feel so... (*He reacts*) Cor! What a hairy 'and you've got, Grannie! (*He opens his eyes and looks down at the hairy paw, then at the hairy arm, then at the hairy chest and finally at the hairy face*)

The Werewolf gives a deep, menacing growl

Reggie drops the paw, screams at the top of his lungs, and runs out DR

The Werewolf growls and snarls at the audience, then bounds out DL

A slight pause

Sternum and Gertrude enter from DR

She is clinging to his arm and being all soppy and romantic. He wears his bowler and is doing his best to retain his butler's dignity while dealing with Gertrude and worrying about the Prince. They move C

Gertrude (*gazing up at him and sighing*) Oh, Mr Sternum, don't you think moonlight is ever so romantic?
Sternum (*deadpan*) Yes, Miss.
Gertrude It makes me go all goose-pimply inside! Does it do the same for you, Mr Sternum?
Sternum (*as before*) Yes, Miss.
Gertrude Mr Sternum?
Sternum Yes, Miss.
Gertrude Are you attached?
Sternum (*puzzled*) Attached, Miss? I believe all my anatomical attributes are in correct accordance with each other, Miss.
Gertrude (*giggling*) No, silly! I mean—do you 'ave a lady friend?
Sternum My duties leave me little time for diversions, Miss.

Gertrude (*to the audience*) Then I'm in with a chance, girls! (*To him, cuddling closer*) Wouldn't you *like* to 'ave one?

Sternum (*after clearing his throat*) May I require how much further it is to your place of residence, Miss. The hour is late, and I am sure you are anxious to retire for the night.

Gertrude Oh, don't worry about that! I'm in no 'urry to get 'ome. (*Snuggling up to him*) I could go on walkin' with you for ever, Mr Sternum.

Sternum Your attentions are very flattering, Miss, but I am most anxious to return to my Master before——

Howling is heard. Both react

(*In anguish*) Oh, calamity! I fear it is too late!

With a snarl, the Werewolf leaps on from DL

Gertrude screams and hides behind Sternum. The Werewolf crouches and growls at them

(*To Werewolf, tentatively*) Your Highness...? Is that you?

Sternum takes a step nearer with Gertrude in tow. The Werewolf springs forward with a snarl. They quickly back away. The Werewolf crouches again

Count De Cash enters from DR, *unseen*

He retreats at the sight of the Werewolf, but curiosity gets the better of him and he remains to observe and listen

(*To Werewolf*) It's... It's Sternum, your Highness... (*He takes a step nearer*) May I suggest that we——

Again the Werewolf springs forward with a snarl. They back away

The Werewolf gives a howl, and bounds out DL

(*In torment*) Oh! My poor Prince Rupert!

Reaction from Gertrude and the Count

Gertrude Eh?!! Prince Rupert! D'you mean that 'orrible 'airy thing is our Prince Rupert?!

Sternum (*sadly*) I regret to say it is, Miss!

Gertrude But... How...? Why...?

Sternum One night, during our travels, the Prince and I were attacked by savage wolves. One of the creatures had the effrontery to bite His Royal Highness on the—ahhem!—nether regions. The following night there was a full moon! Before my very eyes, the Prince changed into—*a werewolf!*

Gertrude Oh, ur!!

Count De Cash steps forward with his mocking laugh. The others react at seeing him

Count Oh, dear! Oh, dear! Your pwecious Pwince is half doggie, eh! How unfowtunate! I suppose we shall have to call him *Pwince Fido* fwom now on! Haw! Haw! Haw!

Sternum (*bristling*) I see no cause for jocularity!

Count Don't you? Well, *I* do! The putwid peasants have been waiting for their Pwince to weturn. All they had to do was whistle or thwow a stick! Haw! Haw! Haw! (*He moves away, laughing*)

Gertrude What are you goin' to do, Mr Sternum?

Sternum It is imperative that the Townsfolk be told of Prince Rupert's condition. Unenlightened, they may attempt to destroy the werewolf!

Count (*turning, struck by a brilliant idea*) Exactly!! And I will help them!

Reaction from the others

(*To the audience*) Oh, this is pe'fect! (*He calls*) Men!!

Cringe and Cower enter DL

Seize these pe'sons immediately!

Cringe and Cower seize Sternum and Gertrude

Sternum I must protest!

Count (*mockingly*) Pwotest all you please, it will make no difference! (*To Cringe and Cower*) take them to the Palace and lock them in the deepest dungeon! (*With a flick of his hanky*) Away with them!

Cringe and Cower haul the protesting Sternum and Gertrude out DL

(*To the audience*) Haw! Haw! Egad! This is indeed most fortunate! My pwoblem of how to dispose of Pwince Wupert is solved. The stupid peasants will be only too eager to help me kill a werewolf! Thus, they will be unwittingly destwoying their own Woyal Pwince, and I shall be fwee to wule Pantovia for ever! Haw! Haw! Haw!

Amid boos and hisses the Count struts off DR, *as the Lights fade to Black-out*

Horror film type music to cover the scene change

SCENE 5

The Town Square

As Act I, Scene 1. Moonlight effect gives the Square a sinister, spooky look. Perhaps a street lamp burns dimly. Some swirling ground mist would add to the effect. The Square is empty

The music fades out. A pause. Howling is heard. Another ominous pause. The audience's attention will be directed at the stage

Silently, the Werewolf enters at the back of the Hall. It prowls about, giving the back rows a fright. It causes havoc as it makes its way through the audience to the stage. At the steps, it turns and snarls at the audience. It has a go at the band, then bounds on to the stage. It howls, and exits R

Yelling is heard off L, *and Reggie runs on from* L *to* C

Reggie (*yelling*) Help! Help—save me! It's after me! Help!

If possible, lights come on in some of the windows

With lots of noise, the Townsfolk rush on from all directions. They wear nightshirts, nightgowns and nightcaps, etc. Rosie and Roxie rush from their house. Roxie wears an outrageous nightgown or pyjama suit with nightcap. She is brandishing an old-fashioned blunderbuss

They all gather around the petrified Reggie

Roxie Reggie Rumple! What on earth's the matter with ya?!
Reggie (*stammering with fright*) M-M-Mum!! I s-s-s-saw it!! (*To the others*) I s-saw it!!
All What?
Reggie Oo!! It was *ghastly*! 'Orrible!! Ooo!!
Roxie Hey! You 'aven't been peepin' through [local person]'s window again, 'ave ya?! I told you about that before!
Reggie It was *'uge*, *'orrible* an' *'airy*!! It 'ad great big pointed teeth, an' claws, an' ...

Rosie What did you see, Reggie?
Reggie (*unable to say the word*) It was a were ... a were ... a were...
Roxie A whirlpool?

Gasping, Reggie shakes his head

A Wurlitzer?

Reggie shakes his head

A curlywurly?

He shakes his head

Oh, I give up! I don't care what it were!
Rosie (*to Reggie*) Try taking a deep breath.

He does so

Now tell us what you saw.
Reggie It was *a werewolf*!

The Townsfolk jeer and laugh

Roxie (*rounding on him*) Oh, you dozy dunder'ead! Fancy getting' everyone
out of bed with a load o' codswallop like that! Oh, you don't 'alf show me
up! You *are* the weakest link—goodbye!
Reggie But it's *true*, Mum! I *did* see a werewolf! I did!

The others laugh and jeer

Roxie You'll see the back of my 'and in a minute!
Reggie (*to the audience*) You saw it as well, didn't you, folks?!

"Yes!" from the audience

Roxie (*to the audience*) Oh, come on! I know 'e's daft, but I expected better
things from you! (*She points someone out*) Especially [name] down there!
There's no such thing as werewolves!
Reggie (*encouraging the audience*) Oh, yes, there is!
Others Oh, no, there isn't!

Routine with the audience follows

During this, the Werewolf enters from R, *unseen*

It joins in and growls "Oh, yes, there is!" a couple of times. Reggie spots the Werewolf and points at it in mute terror. The others stop shouting and look to where he's pointing. They all see the Werewolf, turn back, then do a huge double take. The Werewolf snarls and growls at them. They all scream and rush L, *where they huddle in a terrified group. The Werewolf slowly advances on them*

First Man (*to Roxie*) You've got a gun! Shoot it!
Others (*pushing Roxie*) Shoot it!! Shoot it!!

They push Roxie out into the middle, where she just shivers and shakes. The Werewolf snarls. Roxie yells and retreats. The others push her back with cries of "Shoot it! Kill it!", etc. Trembling, Roxie lifts the blunderbuss, points it at the Werewolf and fires. There is a loud report, lots of smoke and Roxie falls over. The Werewolf is completely unaffected. All watch in mute amazement as it nonchalantly smoothes down its chest fur. It even gives a wolfish laugh. The others gasp in awe

The Werewolf gives a howl, then bounds out R

The others rush to Roxie and help her up. One Man goes R *and looks off*

Man It's going into the wood!
Reggie Now do you believe me, Mum?
Roxie Oh, yes! Oo! I 'aven't seen anythin' so 'orrible since yer Father tried to grow a beard!
Rosie But what *is* a werewolf?
Second Man It's a person who has been bitten by a wolf. Most of the time they're perfectly normal, but at the first sign of a full moon, they change into a savage, blood-thirsty beast!
Roxie (*to Rosie*) Yer father was just like that when 'e saw the full moon! (*She pauses slightly*) Or *any* pub, come to that!
First Woman But what are we going to do?
Second Woman We could all be slaughtered in our beds with that monster on the loose!

Count De Cash enters L

Roxie (*seeing him*) Talkin' of monsters!
Count Gweetings! You seem twoubled. Can I be of any assistance?
Roxie No, thanks! We've 'ad one shock tonight already!

Count Let me guess. You have all seen—the werewolf?
Others Yes!
Count So have I. A loathsome cweature indeed! Our beloved countwy will never be safe as long as it is allowed to woam fwee! As your wuler—and fwiend—it is my duty to organize a hunt. We will wun this foul monster to earth and destwoy it!

The Townsfolk cheer

Are you with me?
Others Aye! Aye!
Roxie Just a minute, Madam Speaker! 'Ow exactly are you gonna kill it? (*She holds up her gun*) I didn't even dent its dog end with this!

The others agree

Count Fear not! I have knowledge of these matters. The only sure way to kill a werewolf is with—a silver bullet! (*He calls*) Men!

Cringe and Cower stagger on from L. They are loaded down with several muskets apiece

The others react

Each of these muskets is loaded with a silver bullet. One well-aimed shot and it's goodbye to the werewolf! (*Quick aside to the audience*) And to Pwince Wupert! (*Aloud to Footmen*) Hand them out!

Cringe and Cower hand the muskets out to the others. During this, the Count comes forward and speaks to the audience

Haw! Haw! The stupid fools! Little do they realize that they will be killing their own pwecious Pwince!
Roxie (*coming down to him with her musket*) Oy! 'Owe come you 'aven't got one of these?
Count I have a small one!
Roxie That's *not* what I was askin'!

The Count takes out a fancy pistol

Count (*to all*) Come, fellow Pantovians! To the wood! The hunt is on! Death to the werewolf!
All (*waving guns*) Death to the werewolf!!

Song 8

This should be a stirring call-to-arms hunting song with a march. The Townsfolk shoulder their muskets and do a march formation us. Comic business with Roxie, Reggie and Cringe and Cower getting into a hopeless tangle with their muskets. The number ends with a tableau, and——

—the Curtain *falls*

ACT II

SCENE 1

The Wood, That Night and the Next Morning

The side wings, ground row and backcloth show a leafy wood. At the back, L, *is a cave entrance. There is a fallen tree trunk* ULC. *Moonlight effect*

After the Entr'acte, the Townsfolk are heard singing in the far distance

Song 8a—Reprise of Song 8

At CURTAIN *rise, the wood is empty and looks creepy in the moonlight. Ground mist swirls. The singing continues at a distance, off* R

Suddenly the Werewolf leaps on to the stage from the top of the cave

It prowls about, snarling and growling at the audience. The singing gets nearer

The Werewolf reacts to this and bounds into the cave

Led by Count De Cash, Rosie, Cringe, Cower and the Townsfolk march on R, *still wearing night attire and shouldering their muskets they march* C, *singing lustily. They form ranks, face front and sing*

Then they march around the stage and out L. *The singing fades away into silence*

The Werewolf emerges from the cave. It sniffs the air

Roxie (*off* R, *calling*) Yooo hooo! Where are yooo?!
Reggie (*off* L, *calling back*) I'm over here! Where are yooohooo?!

The Werewolf growls, rubs its belly hungrily, then disappears back into the cave

Simultaneously, Roxie creeps on backwards from R, *as Reggie creeps on backwards from* L

Both are scared. Roxie wears a ludicrous safari outfit with sola topi and baggy shorts. Reggie is wearing an ill-fitting hunting costume with riding hat, red coat and "wired out" breeches. Comic business as they circle each other, back to back. Eventually their bottoms touch. They freeze in terror, then slowly turn to face each other

Roxie Oh, it's only you, Reggie! Thank goodness! I thought I was 'avin' a close encounter of the *furred* kind! Me whole life flashed before me! All twenty-five years of it!

Reggie Where's Rosie and the others?

Roxie I dunno! I lost 'em. I stopped to adjust me polar trophy and when I turned round, they'd disappeared!

Reggie I became detached as well!

Roxie (*eyeing his breeches*) Yes, I'm not surprised, wearin' those! Tell me, are these the latest thing from Top Man, or 'ave you just 'ad an accident?

Comic business as Reggie does a funny walk in the breeches. He flaps the sides, etc.

That's enough, Dumbo! You'll take off in a minute!

Reggie I wonder what's 'appened to them, Mum? (*Scared*) Y-You don't think the w-werewolf got 'em, do you?!

They look about, scared. Roxie turns away from Reggie

It might 'ave pounced on 'em from the undergrowth! (*He snarls and pounces on Roxie*)

Roxie (*yelling with fright*) Yaaaah!! Oh, you great steamin' nit! I'll pounce on *your* undergrowth in a minute! Now, stop talkin' like that. (*With false bravado*) Your sister and the others are perfectly safe.

Reggie Yeah—We'd 'ave 'eard the screams.

Roxie (*gulping*) The s-screams?

Reggie Yeah! The agonizin' screams as it tore them to pieces an' chewed 'em up!

Roxie (*shuddering*) Ugggh!!

Reggie On what day of the week do werewolves eat people?

Roxie (*timidly*) I dunno.

Reggie *Chews*day! (*He guffaws*)

Roxie (*grabbing him by his lapels*) Listen, Willie Carson [or other jockey]! Any more cracks like that, an' I'll jab you in yer jodhpurs! (*She releases*

him) They can't be far away. I know! Let's ask our friends out there. (*She indicates the audience*)

Reggie (*peering out*) Are you sure they're still 'ere? The werewolf might 'ave scared 'em off!

Roxie I'll check! (*To the audience, calling*) Are you still there?!!

"Yes!" from the audience

(*To Reggie*) Yes, they're all there.

Reggie I'm not sure about that, Mum. (*He points to someone*) 'E's definitely not—*all there*! (*He guffaws*)

Roxie takes a swing at him. He ducks away and repeats the funny walk

Roxie (*to the audience*) Ignore 'im! 'Is father spent a lot of time in [local place]! Now, 'ave you seen our Rosie and the others?

"Yes!" from the audience

Reggie (*to the audience*) Did they come this way?

"Yes!" from the audience

Roxie Which way did they go?

Business with the audience giving them directions. Reggie thanks them, ad lib

Reggie C'mon, Mum! Let's catch 'em up! Walk this way! (*He does a funny walk to the exit L*)

Roxie Oh, I'm too shattered to go another step at this time of night! I should be tucked up in bed with [popular male author]! They'll be back in a minute. Let's sit down an' wait. (*She sits at the R end of a tree trunk*)

Reggie But, Mum... The werewolf!

Roxie Oh, it'll be miles away by now. It's probably spendin' the night at the [local hotel]! They do four star doggie bags! Come and sit down!

Reggie sits at the L end of the tree trunk. They face front

Reggie Do you really think it's gone away, Mum?

Roxie (*confidently*) Miles away!

Pause, as the Werewolf emerges from the cave

The audience will be shouting, but Roxie and Reggie take no notice

Reggie And we've got nothing to worry about?
Roxie (*confidently*) Absolutely nothin'!

Pause, as the Werewolf moves down between them and eyes them hungrily

Reggie But what if it comes back, Mum?
Roxie It won't!

The Werewolf climbs over the trunk and sits down between them. All three are facing front. The following sequence is done without a word spoken. Simultaneously, Roxie and Reggie cross their legs. The Werewolf copies them. Pause. All three sigh, then re-cross their legs. Pause. All three sigh, then uncross their legs. The Werewolf starts sniffing Roxie. Annoyed, she takes out a large handkerchief and hands it across to Reggie. The Werewolf takes it and blows its nose into it loudly. It hands it on to Reggie. Puzzled, Reggie opens the handkerchief. It has a large hole in the middle. The Werewolf sniffs Reggie. At this point Reggie surreptitiously switches the handkerchief, and hands it across to Roxie. The Werewolf takes it and blows its nose. It hands it on to Roxie. She opens it to discover that it is now in shreds. Annoyed, she puts it away

I wish they'd 'urry up an' come back! (*She shivers*) Brr! It's flippin' freezin' sittin' out 'ere in just me short shorts! (*She shivers again*) Brr!!

The Werewolf puts its arm around her shoulder

Oh, thanks, son. (*She shuts her eyes and snuggles up to the Werewolf*) Oo! That's better. You're just like a warm fur coat!

Puzzled, Reggie looks towards Roxie. He sees the Werewolf and slowly rises in mute terror. He just stands there gaping and pointing

(*Rambling on, blissfully unaware*) Y'know, when you were a little tiny tot I used to cuddle *you* up like this. All nice an' cosy. (*She reaches up and strokes the Werewolfs's claw*) Oh Reggie! I do wish you'd take better care of yer fingernails. They're all... (*She opens her eyes and sees the claw, then the furry face. She gulps*)

The Werewolf gives a deep growl

Roxie & Reggie Aahhhhgh!!!

Startled, the Werewolf lets go of Roxie. She leaps up and runs around the stage, yelling at the top of her lungs. Reggie does the same. The Werewolf just sits there, watching them in total amazement

The Werewolf then shrugs, gets up and lopes off R

Roxie and Reggie continue to charge around. Finally, they collide and fall to the ground, where they wrestle with each other

Roxie & Reggie It's got me!! It's got me!!

Rosie, Count De Cash, Cringe, Cower and the Townsfolk rush on from L

Rosie Mum…! Reggie…!

Roxie and Reggie continue to wrestle with each other. Rosie wades in and pulls them apart. They stagger to their feet, still panic-stricken

Roxie & Reggie Where is it?! Where is it?!
Rosie Calm down. We're here. You're safe now.
Roxie Oh, it was 'ere! The herewolf was weare!!
Count Which way did it go?
Roxie (*wailing*) We don't know!
Reggie (*wailing even louder*) And we don't care!!
Count (*to all, pointing* R) It must have gone that way! Follow me! Death to the werewolf!
Others (*waving muskets*) Death to the werewolf!!

The Count rushes to the exit R, *followed by all the others, chanting "Death to the Werewolf!". At the exit he pauses and lets the others rush out*

The Count turns to the audience

Count Yes! Death to the werewolf! And—death to Pwince Wupert!!

Amid boos and hisses, the Count exits R

The chanting fades away into silence

The Werewolf lopes on L

It doesn't snarl or growl this time. It stretches its arms and gives a couple of big yawns

The Werewolf lumbers up to the cave, gives another yawn and disappears inside

Soon loud growly snores are heard, then silence. The Lights fade to Black-out

A pause

Dawn chorus of bird song is heard. "Morning" from Grieg's "Peer Gynt" suite is played. Lighting effect of the dawn coming up. Soon the wood is filled with bright morning sunshine

Small animals, such as rabbits, squirrels, etc. enter the scene. Colourful birds and butterflies appear. The music changes and they all perform a charming dance

Song 9

After the dance, voices are heard off stage R

The Wildlife scatter and exit in all directions

Cringe and Cower lumber on from R, *without muskets. Both are tired and weary*

Cringe (*to the audience*) Cor! All last night we were trampin' around this wood!

Cower Yeah! And not a wink of sleep! I can 'ardly keep me eyes open! (*He gives an enormous yawn*)

Cringe Oy! Stop that! You'll start *them* off! (*He indicates the audience*) And I don't think some of 'em need much encouragement.

Cower Well, at least the werewolf got away. (*Gleefully*) Cor! That really got up old face-ache's nose!

Cringe Yeah! 'E's hoppin' mad! And by now the Prince should be back to normal. There's only one problem. As soon as he changes back into a werewolf old smarty pants will 'ave everyone out tryin' to kill 'im again! We've got to do somethin'!

Cower (*enthused*) Yeah! (*Dumbly*) Wot?

Cringe Listen. The townsfolk don't know that the werewolf is really Prince Rupert, do they? If they *did* they wouldn't let old niggle knickers kill him, would they?

Cower That's true. Who's gonna tell 'em?

Cringe We are!

Cower Good! (*He reacts*) Eh?!!

Cringe It's the only way.

Cower But what if Mr Nasty finds out? 'E'll 'ave our guts for garters!

Cringe By the time 'e does, the Prince will 'ave taken over, 'e'll be in jail and we will be national heroes!

Cower (*puffing his chest*) Yeah! Just like [topical or local personality]!

Cringe We might get decorated!

Cower Yeah! The best that [local DIY shop or decorating firm] can supply!

Cringe No, you foolish flunky! I mean we might get a medal or even—*a knighthood*!

Cower Yeah! A knighthood—with matching accessories! (*He parades about, then is struck by a sobering thought*) Just a minute! You've forgotten somethin'—the Prince will still be a werewolf!

Cringe No problem! I'm sure a trip to Dr [local] will sort him out.

Cower Oh, 'e's *ever* so good! 'E cured my uncle when 'e thought 'e was a pair of curtains.

Cringe What did 'e do?

Cower 'E told 'im to stop 'angin' about and pull 'imself together!

Cringe C'mon! Let's tell the others before Slippery Sam turns up!

Cower and Cringe rush to exit R, but pull up short as Count De Cash enters there

Count Ah!

Cringe & Cower (*backing away*) Aahhh!

Count What are you loitewing here for? Get back to the palace and pwepare my breakfast! (*He dismisses them with a flick of his handkerchief and comes forward to speak to the audience*)

Cringe and Cower hover US, nervously

(*To the audience*) How fwightfully vexing! The wetched werewolf escaped last night! I suppose that pleases you, eh?

The audience responds

Well, enjoy your mewiment while you can, wiff waff! Because tonight I will have another chance! Oh, yes! As luck would have it— (*archly*) and for the sake of the plot—there is to be another full moon! Haw! Haw! Pwince Wupert will once again become a werewolf and this time I will destwoy him! Oh, yes, I will!

Routine with the audience. Cringe and Cower move down and join in with the "Oh, no, you won'ts". Eventually the Count becomes aware of them. He stops his banter with the audience and moves over to Cringe and Cower, threateningly. They dwindle into silence

So! What is this! Webellion! Are you wevolting, you wevolting wetainers?

Cringe (*still scared, but standing up to him*) Y-Yes! We are wevolting!

Cower (*going right up to the Count*) An' so are woo ... er ... *you*! (*He sticks his tongue out, then quickly hides behind Cringe*) Go on! Tell 'im!

Cringe (*gulping, then all in one breath*) Royal Rupert's really the rightful ruler to reign regally and you're rotten rubbish!

Cower Cor! That was good! Say it again!

Cringe You must be jokin'!

Count (*with his mocking laugh*) Haw! Haw! How touching! And what *may* I ask, do you intend to do about it? (*He turns away slightly*)

Cringe We're gonna tell everyone the truth about the werewolf!

Cower And why you *really* want to kill it!

Count (*spinning round with his pistol drawn*) I think not!!

With a yell, Cringe and Cower shoot their arms into the air. Their knees knock with fright

Haw! Haw! Haw! Not so webellious now, what! (*Viciously*) You scum will not be telling anyone anything! You will be joining those other fools in my dungeon! (*To the audience*) You see! No-one can outsmart me! Tonight I will kill Pwince Wupert as planned! (*To Cringe and Cower*) Now—*move*!! (*He gestures to the exit* L *with his pistol*)

Whimpering and still holding their hands up, Cringe and Cower exit L. *The Count follows, laughing his mocking laugh*

Prince Rupert emerges sleepily from the cave. He stretches, rubs his eyes, then looks about him in utter amazement

Rupert What... What on earth am I doing in this wood? I don't remember coming here! I was asleep in that cave! How did I get there?! Oh, this is very weird—the last thing I remember was talking to Rosie's mother after the party—the rest is a complete blank! What's wrong with me? Why can't I remember? (*He sits on the tree trunk and puts his head in his hands*)

A Rabbit hops on

It looks at Rupert, quizzically, then beckons off

More Animals creep on. Soon all the Wildlife has emerged

They move tentatively towards Rupert. Suddenly he lifts his head and the frightened Animals retreat

Oh, please don't be frightened. I'm not going to hurt you. (*He holds out his hand*) Come on, there's nothing to be afraid of. I just want to be your friend.

Song 10

As Rupert sings, the Wildlife move in closer and closer. Soon he is making friends with them all. Finally, they join him in a dance routine. The music continues under the following dialogue

And now, my new-found friends, I must bid you farewell. I have to find my way out of this wood and back to my darling Rosie.

Rupert goes to exit R, turns to wave to the Animals, then exits

They wave back. The music comes up and the Wildlife perform a short reprise of the No. 10 dance. It ends with a tableau, as the Lights fade to Black-out

Music to cover the scene change

SCENE 2

A Dungeon

Tabs or a front-cloth showing dank slimy walls with a skeleton hanging in chains, etc. Gloomy Lighting

Gertrude and Sternum are discovered. She is seated on a small, rough bench
C. *He is pacing up and down in an agitated manner. Despite the situation, Gertrude is obviously enjoying being in close confinement with Sternum. Eventually he goes to the DL exit and calls*

Sternum Hallo! Hallo!
Gertrude (*singing*) "Who's your lady friend..."

Sternum gives her a sharp look. She giggles. He resumes calling

Sternum Can you hear me out there?! If you do not release us immediately I shall be forced to take the matter up with [local councillor or MP]! Hallo! (*Frustrated, he turns away*) Oh, botheration!! (*He resumes pacing*)
Gertrude You're wastin' your time. Mr Sternum. 'E's not gonna let us out.

We know too much. (*Patting the small space beside her*) Why don't you come and sit down.

Sternum No, thank you, Miss. I have no desire to prostrate myself at the moment.

Gertrude I wasn't askin' you to do *that*! I just asked you to sit down.

Sternum I am much too concerned about His Royal Highness. I have no indication whether the poor young gentleman is alive or dead!

Gertrude Look, if 'e was dead, De Cash would 'ave been in 'ere gloatin' about it. I'm sure the Prince is alive an' well.

Sternum Thank you for your solace, Miss.

Gertrude (*very pleased*) Not at all. Don't mention it. You're welcome. (*To the audience*) Wos a solace?

Sternum (*near tears*) Oh, my poor young Prince! I have failed him! I should now be at his side, instead of dallying in this despicable despot's dungeon!

Gertrude Well, there's nothin' you can do about it. We've just got to make the best of things. Come and sit down.

Sternum sighs and sits beside her. It is a very tight squeeze

There! Are you comfy?

Sternum (*anything but*) Ecstatically, Miss.

Gertrude You could 'ave a lot worse company than me, y'know.

Sternum I concede that to be correct, Miss.

Gertrude (*angling*) And... And you do like me—just a little bit—don't you?

Sternum (*after clearing his throat*) I must confess that I find a certain congenial aspect in your personality highly acceptable, Miss.

Gertrude Good! (*Still not sure*) Does all that mean you like me?

Sternum Yes, Miss.

Gertrude (*thrilled and snuggling closer*) Ooo! Say— (*In a "sexy" voice*) I like you—Gertrude.

Sternum (*doing his best to copy her*) I like you—Gertrude.

Gertrude (*squirms with delight*) Ooo! An' I like you ... er ... what is your first name, by the way?

Sternum Peregrine.

Gertrude (*stifling her giggles*) Oh, I say! Can I call you Perry!

Sternum You may call me anything you choose providing you don't call me too early in the morning. (*For the first time he actually laughs. Be it rather reserved laughter*)

Gertrude is startled at first, then joins in

Gertrude Oh, Perry! You made a joke! (*Aside to the audience*) Not a very *funny* joke, but it's a start.

Sternum I am glad you appreciated my little quip.
Gertrude We'll discuss your little quip later on. Give me yer 'and!
Sternum (*puzzled*) What do you want it for?
Gertrude (*all soppy*) I wanna hold it!

*Sternum rigidly puts out his hand. Gertrude takes it in hers and caresses it.
He is obviously greatly affected by this, but tries desperately to retain his
decorum*

(*Seductively*) How does that feel? Is it nice? Do you like that, Perry?
Sternum (*stammering, and trying to keep control*) I-I cannot find the words!
Gertrude (*to the audience*) Thank goodness for that! (*To Sternum*) We don't
need words! We need action!

Song 11

*This should be a comic version of a "smouldering" tango. Singing in a deep
"sexy" voice, Gertrude plays up to Sternum in a comic seductive manner. She
wraps herself around him, throws herself across his knees, etc. He withstands
it as long as he can, then loses control and breaks into a song himself. They
dance a "passionate" tango together. It ends with Gertrude bending him
over in a Valentino type embrace*

After the dance, the sound of a heavy door being unlocked is heard off L

Cringe and Cower, still with their hands in the air, enter DL. *They are
followed by Count De Cash, still holding his pistol*

Count (*with his usual mocking laugh*) Gweetings! I have bwought you some
company to share your salubwious suwoundings! They also thought they
could outwit Count De Cash! Haw! Haw! Haw!
Cringe & Cower (*waving lamely to the others with their hands in the air*)
Hallo!
Sternum How dare you keep us imprisoned here! I *demand* that you——
Count Silence! You will demand nothing, you puffed-up waiter!
Sternum (*outraged*) Waiter!! I am the personal manservant of his Royal
Highness, Prince Rupert of Pantovia!
Count (*sneering*) In that case I should have called you a puffed-up *dog
handler*! Haw! Haw!
Sternum (*near to explosion point*) You... You... You're no gentlemen, sir!

*Laughing his mocking laugh and sneering at the audience, the Count
exits* DL

The sound of the door being locked is heard off L. *Cringe lowers his arms and has to nudge Cower to do the same*

(*To Cringe and Cower, earnestly*) Please elucidate on the predicament of my misfortunate Monarch!

Cringe & Cower (*dumbly*) Eh?!!

Gertrude What's 'appened to the Prince?

Cringe Oh! Well, 'e managed to escape from old fancy pants last night…

Cower And as far as we know, 'e's back to normal!

Sternum and Gertrude are overjoyed and embrace each other

Gertrude You see! I told you 'e was all right!

Sternum (*with restrained rapture*) Oh, jubilation!

Cringe (*gloomily*) I wouldn't get too excited though.

Cower No. Unfortunately…

Cringe & Cower (*to the audience, archly*) And for the sake of the plot!

Cringe (*to Sternum and Gertrude*) There's gonna be another full moon tonight!

Cower That means the Prince will start doin' 'is Lassie impressions again!

Cringe An' De Cash will be out tryin' to kill 'im!

Cower With 'is silver bonnet!

Cringe *Bullet*, you twit! (*To the others*) We were gonna tell everyone an' stop it 'appenin'…

Cower But 'e nobbled us!

Gertrude We've got to do somethin'! What time is it now?

Cower Accordin' to my stomach—about teatime!

Sternum That means we only have a few hours in which to prevent the tragedy! We *must* escape!

Others Yes!!

All (*to the audience, melodramatically*) But how?!!

Quick Black-out

Dramatic music to cover the scene change

SCENE 3

Roxie's Keep Fit Class

As Act I, Scene 3, without the party decorations. There is a large sofa at the back. The Werewolf is already concealed behind it. General Lighting

Reggie and Townsfolk are discovered. They look pretty comical in a variety of outfits suitable for keep fit. Reggie looks even more ridiculous in his version of the "Mr Motivator" outfit. Comic business as he takes the others through their warm-up exercises to the accompaniment of the piano

Reggie (*after business*) And—rest!

The Townsfolk don't so much rest as collapse against each other, exhausted! A whistle is heard blowing off L

Get ready, team! Here comes your fitness instructor! Roxie "Aerobics" Rumple!

Roxie springs on L. *She is wearing a brightly-coloured leotard and has her hair tied up. She also wears leg warmers and has a whistle hung around her neck*

She springs up and down across the front of the stage, then touches her toes. She comes over giddy and falls to the floor with a thump

Roxie (*sitting up; to Reggie*) Oy! Mr Rotivator! Don't just stand there—'elp me up!

Reggie does so

(*Aside to him*) I'm a bit out of practice! D'you think they noticed?
Reggie No. (*He points to the floor*) But I bet the woodworm did!
Roxie (*to the Townsfolk, trying to save face*) It's all right, class. I just slipped. Good evening and welcome to "Wriggle it with Roxie". It's so nice to see you all back after last week's little catastrophe.
Reggie Yes. Mr [local person] finds the neck brace very useful as it saves 'im wearin' a scarf. Now, tonight's class will only be a short one. That is because...
Roxie & Reggie (*to the audience, archly*) And for the sake of the plot!
Roxie There's gonna be another full moon! That means our furry friend the werewolf will be on the prowl again, and I know you all want to join in the hunt. Right, then! Let's get active! 'Ave they done their warm-up exercises, Reggie?
Reggie Yes, Mum! They're all heated up an' ready to go!

Roxie surveys the wilting Townsfolk

Roxie Ready to go *where*? The cemetery! (*She blows her whistle at the*

group, making them jump) Come along! Exercise! Exercise! It's the only
way to fight the flab! And as you can see— *(she runs her hands down her
figure)* it worked for me!

Reggie Yeah! All *three* of you! *(He guffaws)*

Roxie Shut it, you! *(To the group)* Come along! *(She claps her hands)* Into
your places!

The Townsfolk form a line across the back. Reggie gets on the end

Now—follow me! Music!!

*Taped exercise class type music played over the sound system. Comic
business as Roxie turns us and takes the Townsfolk through various exercises.
Side bends, toe touching, arm stretches, etc. The back view of Roxie should
guarantee much laughter from the audience. After a while, Reggie comes
down to Roxie and taps her on the bottom as she is touching her toes. Reduce
music volume*

(Clinging to him and gasping for breadth) Wos the matter? ... 'Ad enough
already?

Reggie *(pointing to the audience)* It's that lot, Mum! They keep laughin' at
us!

Roxie Oh, do they! I'll soon sort them out! *(To the audience)* So, you think
it's funny, eh? Well, let's see 'ow good you are at it! Come on! Stand up!
All of you! Up you get! Give Gran a hand! And you lot at the back! *(Ad
lib)*

*The House Lights come up, as Roxie and the others encourage the audience
to stand*

(Surveying them) Well! I don't know what you've got to laugh about! I've
never seen such an unfit load o' layabouts in all my life!

Reggie *(pointing out a group)* Especially *them* over there!

Roxie *(looking)* Oh, yes! The only exercise they get is bendin' their elbows
at the [local pub]! *(To the whole audience)* Right, then! All you 'ave to do
is copy me an' keep in time with the music!

*Increase volume of music. Comic business and participation as Roxie takes
the audience through the exercises. Reggie and the Townsfolk join in. After
a while, the music slows right down, forcing them to do the exercises in slow
motion. Suddenly, it increases to treble its original speed, making them jerk
about uncontrollably. This "fast and slow" business can be repeated as
desired. Eventually, Roxie stops the proceedings and yells to the back of the
hall*

(*Shouting*) All right! All right! You win!!

The taped music stops abruptly

(*To the audience*) 'E's not been the same since we got the electricity! You can all sit down again now. I bet you feel a lot fitter after that. We ought to charge you extra!

The audience resume their seats and the House Lights go down

(*To Townsfolk*) Well, that's the end of tonight's class. You can all go 'ome an' get ready to play hunt the werewolf. See you next week!

The Townsfolk start to hobble out R. *They cling to each other, completely worn out and exhausted. A very sorry-looking bunch*

(*To the audience*) There they go! Every one a perfect specimen of physical fitness!

The Townsfolk hobble out

Reggie starts doing some comical exercises

Hey! Mr Universe [or one of the Gladiators]! We've finished!
Reggie Oh, these are my "cool-down" exercises!
Roxie Looks more like fall-down, to me! Stop messin' about an' go an' get the chocolate bickies!

Rosie enters R. *She looks upset and worried*

(*Going to her*) 'Ello, Rosie! What's up, girl? You've got a face like [local place] on a wet weekend! Where 'ave you been all day?
Rosie I've been looking for Tom. I've searched everywhere and there's no sign of him! Oh, what's happened to him, Mum! (*She starts to cry*)
Roxie (*comforting her*) There! There! Don't upset yerself, love. That's a man all over! Under yer feet one minute, and under starter's orders the next!
Reggie It's strange, though! That butler chap of 'is 'as vanished as well! *And* Gertrude! 'Ere! You don't think the werewolf got 'em, do you!

Rosie wails

Roxie (*to Reggie*) Put a sock in it! (*To Rosie*) Come on, love. Nothin's 'appened to Tom. 'E probably went sightseein' an' got lost.

Rosie (*cheering up a bit*) Do you really think so, Mum?
Roxie Positive! Now, we'd better get ready for the werewolf hunt.

Roxie and Reggie move to the exit L. He stops

Reggie Hey! They could 'ave been viaducted by aliens!
Roxie I'll viaduct you in a minute! Get out!

Roxie pushes Reggie off L, and exits

Rosie (*to the audience*) Oh, I do hope Mum's right. I couldn't bear the
thought of never seeing Tom again. I love him so much, you see. And it's
not just puppy love. It's the real thing.

*To suitable music, a Rabbit hops on from R. It carries a letter. The music
fades out*

Good heavens! Hallo, Mr Rabbit.

The Rabbit bows to her

What are you doing here?

The Rabbit holds out the letter

A letter! Is it for me?

The Rabbit nods its head. Rosie takes the letter

Thank you, Mr Rabbit.

The Rabbit bows to her, then hops to the exit R

Goodbye!

The Rabbit turns and waves to her. It waves to the audience, then hops out R

(*Opening the letter*) I wonder if it's from Tom! (*She looks at it*) No, it's
from Grannie! (*She reads*) "Dear nearest and dearest, and all those who
hope to be remembered in my will. I hope this leaves you as it finds me.
I am writing this very slowly as I know you can't read very fast. I am not
feeling myself at the moment because I am in bed with (*she turns the letter
over*) a nasty cold. Help wanted. Come at once. PS the pedal bin needs

emptying and there is an awful smell from your loving Gran". Oh, dear! Poor old Grannie's ill! We must go to her at once! (*She drops the letter on the sofa, goes to the exit* L *and calls*) Mum! Reggie!

No reply

Oh, they can't hear me! I'll have to go on my own. I suppose I'd better wear the red riding hood or Grannie'll be upset. (*Quickly*) Oh, dear. What a shame. It's not here.

A hand appears from the wings, holding out the red riding hood. Rosie reacts and takes it, contemptuously

(*To the wings*) Thanks! I'll do *you* a favour one day!

Putting on the riding hood, Rosie hurries out R

Roxie and Reggie enter L. *Both wear smock like outfits that can easily be slipped over their keep fit gear. These are made from camouflage material and have matching hats shaped like helmets*

Roxie Yes, what is it, Rosie? Oh, she's not 'ere!
Reggie Probably out lookin' fer lover boy again!
Roxie Well, I 'ope she's back before the full moon! We should all stick together when the werewolf's on the prowl!

Rupert enters R

Rupert (*moving* DR) Hallo!

Roxie and Reggie react

Roxie 'Ello! 'Ello! Is that all you've got to say for yerself, young man! Our Rosie's worried witless about you! She's been out all day lookin' for ya! Where've ya been?
Rupert I'm awfully sorry. It's very strange. I woke up this morning in the middle of a wood! I haven't got the foggiest idea how I got there. It's most odd!
Reggie (*taking Roxie aside* DL) I reckon 'e's been on the [local brew]!
Rupert It's taken me all day to find my way out of the wretched wood! Is Rosie here?
Roxie No! She's gone out lookin' for you again!
Rupert Well, as soon as she returns, I have a very important announcement to make.

The full moon effect is seen through the window

Roxie You said that last night.
Rupert Did I...? (*He falters, puts his hand to his head and starts to sway*).
   I ... I seem to remember ... remember...

As in Act I, Scene 3, Rupert turns to look at the moon and becomes strangely affected. Roxie and Reggie watch gobsmacked as he goes through the business of scratching, pulling at his clothes, etc., etc. He goes down on all fours, bounds US and drops out of sight behind the sofa. Roxie and Reggie gape at each other, then at the audience. They remain facing out front

Roxie You're right! 'E *'as* been on the [local brew]!

Strange gurgles and growls are heard coming from behind the sofa

Reggie It certainly sounds like it!

More gurgles, growls and thrashing about noises are heard

Roxie Either that or 'e's 'ad a dinner at [local school]!

The sounds stop. Slowly the furry claws of the werewolf appear over the back of the sofa—then the furry head! The audience will be shouting "Behind you!", etc.

   (*To the audience*) You what? Behind us? What's behind us?

"The Werewolf!" from the audience

Reggie The werewolf? In our 'ouse?! Don't talk rubbish! Oh, no, it isn't!

Routine with the audience

Roxie (*to Reggie*) I know what we'll do. We'll count to three, then turn
   round!
Roxie & Reggie One—two—*three*!!

They turn to look, but the Werewolf has dropped out of sight. They face front, and the Werewolf appears again. The counting business can be repeated as desired. On the last time, the Werewolf does not re-appear

Roxie (*to the audience*) I knew it! You were just 'avin' us on! Well, it didn't
   work!

Reggie (*to the audience*) No! You can "full monty" but you can't fool *us*!
Roxie There's no werewolf behind us! It's just our Rosie's boyfriend with a 'angover!

They go up and stand at each end of the sofa. They don't look behind it

Come on out, Tom! What you need is the 'air of the dog!

The Werewolf rises up in full view

(*Looking at it, absently*) Oh, I see you've already got it!

Roxie and Reggie do a huge double take. The Werewolf growls and snarls at them. Screaming, they run around the room, pursued by the monster

Eventually, the Werewolf bounds off R, *leaving them in a trembling, wailing heap*

Count De Cash rushes on R, *with his pistol at the ready. He is followed by the Townsfolk, now dressed and armed with muskets*

Count Was it the werewolf?!
Roxie & Reggie (*wailing*) Yes!!
Count Which way did it go?

Roxie and Reggie just point R, *with shaking fingers*

(*To the others*) After it! Death to the werewolf!!
Others (*waving muskets*) Death to the werewolf!!

The Count rushes out R, *followed by the Townsfolk*

Reggie Mum! Don't you realize! Our Rosie's Tom *is the werewolf*!!
Roxie I know! Oh, this is terrible! 'Ow am I gonna tell 'er! Oh, my poor little girl! In love with a ... *a dogsbody*!!

Reggie finds the letter

Reggie Hey! Look! It's a letter from Gran!
Roxie Oh, what does she want at a time like this!
Reggie (*after a quick scan of the letter*) She's ill an' askin' for 'elp! I bet Rosie's gone to 'er cottage!
Roxie (*in horror*) Oh, no!! My baby girl! Alone in that wood with a lerewolf

on the woose! We've got to find 'er before she ends up as a tin of Pedigree Chum!

Roxie grabs Reggie and drags him out R

Quick Black-out

Horror film style music to cover the scene change

SCENE 4

The Path Near the Wood

As Act I, Scene 2. Spooky Lighting and full moon effect on front-cloth

Howling is heard. A pause

Rosie enters timidly from DR *and moves* C

Rosie Oh, dear! I've never been into the wood after dark before. I ... I must confess to being a little bit scared.

Howling is heard. Rosie jumps with fright

J-Just a little bit. Oh, I wish Tom were here! I wouldn't be afraid of anything if he were beside me. Oh, Tom! Where are you?

Song 12

After the song, howling is heard. Rosie reacts with fear, and runs to the exit DR. *She stops*

No! I *mustn't* go back! (*She moves back* C) Poor old Grannie's ill and needs my help. I mustn't let her down. But why couldn't she live in [local sheltered housing] instead of this creepy wood!

Rosie exits DL

A slight pause

The Werewolf lopes on DR. *It points in Rosie's direction, then points to its mouth. It rubs its belly hungrily, then bounds off* DL

Chanting of "Death to the Werewolf!" is heard

Count De Cash enters DR, *followed by the Townsfolk. They march across and exit* DL

Roxie *(off* DR; *calling timidly)* Rosie! ... W-W-Where are you?

Roxie and Reggie creep on DR. *Both are very scared*

Reggie Oo, Mum! Do we 'ave to do this now? Couldn't we find Rosie in the mornin'?
Roxie You stupid boy! By the mornin' there might not be any Rosie *to* find! *(Gulping)* Except a pile of bones!
Reggie And some lumps of gristle!
Roxie & Reggie *(shuddering)* Ugggh!!

Howling is heard. They jump with fright and cling to each other

Roxie W-W-What w-was that?!
Reggie 'Owls!
Roxie Owls? But they go "too wit to woo", don't they?
Reggie Not *owls*! 'Owls! Werewolf 'owls!!
Roxie Ooo! *(She looks* R *and reacts in horror)* Ahhh! W-What's *that*?! Over there!!
Reggie *(looking and gulping)* Th-There's s-s-something movin' about ... Oh, no! It's comin' this way!! *(He buries his face in Roxie's bosom)*
Roxie *(OTT)* This is it, Reggie! We're goin' to join yer father in heaven— or the other place! Ooo!! *(She clings to him with her eyes shut)*

Unseen by them, Sternum enters DR. *He moves over to them and does his butler's cough*

An' 'e's still got that cough, by the sound of it! It'll be the death of 'im!
Sternum Good evening, Madam.

Roxie and Reggie react, then see Sternum

Reggie Hey! It's Scrotum—or whatever 'is name is!

Gertrude enters DR, *followed by Cringe and Cower*

Gertrude Mrs Rumple! Reggie!
Roxie It's Gertrude—and the two sticks of celery! But... What's goin' on?!

Gertrude Oh, you'll never believe it!

Roxie Believe what? An' if it's a long story, don't let (*she indicates Sternum*) *'im* tell it!

Gertrude Well, to begin with—Prince Rupert 'as returned!

Roxie & Reggie (*delighted*) Oh!

Gertrude But 'e's the werewolf!

Roxie & Reggie (*disappointed*) Oh!

Roxie (*reacting*) Eh?!! But… But the werewolf is Rosie's boyfriend! Only she doesn't know 'e's a werewolf!

Cringe No-one does—except us and Count De Cash! 'E found out about the Prince and wants 'im dead!

Cower We tried to stop 'im, but 'e got wind——

Roxie Serve 'im right!

Cower —of our plan.

Sternum He incarcerated us!

Reggie Cor! Painful!

Cringe (*to the audience*) I bet you're all dyin' to know how we escaped from the dungeon. (*To Cower*) Tell 'em!

Cower (*to the audience, really building it up*) We managed to effect our daring escape by means of— (*he produces a key*) this key! (*Very matter of factly*) I forgot I 'ad a spare one in my pocket.

Roxie That's not a very excitin' escape story, is it?!

Cringe What do you expect—[current action adventure film or TV programme]?

Sternum It is imperative that we find His Royal Highness before any harm befalls him. He must be protected!

Roxie But 'e's a werewolf! 'Ow do you protect a werewolf?

Reggie Give 'im a Bob Martins?

Gertrude We'll do what we were goin' to do in the first place! Tell the others who the werewolf is. They won't want to 'elp De Cash kill Prince Rupert.

The others agree

Cringe (*to the audience*) Folks, did you see which way old fancy pants an' the others went?

The audience give him directions

Thanks, folks! (*To the others*) What are we waitin' for!

Cringe rushes out DL, *followed by Cower, Sternum and Gertrude*

Roxie is about to follow, but sees Reggie hanging back

Roxie Come on!
Reggie I-I'll stay 'ere and look for Rosie.

Howling is heard. Reggie jumps with fright

On second thoughts!!

Reggie runs out DL. *Roxie follows, as the Lights fade to Black-out*

Music to cover the scene change

SCENE 5

Grannie's Cottage in the Wood

*Side wings and back wall represent a room in a quaint, but tumbledown
cottage. Painted on the flats are pictures, a mirror, fireplace and curtained
window, etc. In the centre of the back wall is a practical door. A broom leans
against the wall* R. *An old-fashioned iron bedstead with pillows, sheets and
patchwork quilt is* LC, *with its left side facing the audience. Below the bed
head is a small table with a medicine bottle and a box of pills. General
Lighting*

*Grannie Grabbit is discovered, sitting up in bed. She is wearing a nightgown,
shawl and filly nightcap. A spare nightcap hangs on the bedpost. Her glasses
are perched on her forehead. She is suffering from a cold and is coughing and
sneezing*

Grannie (*sneezing*) Achoooo!! Lummy! I nearly lost me top set that time!
   Drat this bloomin' cold! And I wanted to go jitterbuggin' at [local teenage
   nightspot]'s tonight too! I'd better try some of this jollop, I suppose! (*She
   takes the pill box from the table. She has great difficulty trying to read the
   instructions on the box*) Oh, confound it! I wish I could find me specs! I
   dunno what's 'appened to 'em! (*She tries reading the box again*) Now! Is
   it one tablet six times a day, or six tablets once a day?! Newfangled rubbish!
   I'll try one of me own remedies! (*She puts the box on the table and climbs
   out of bed. She is still wearing her boots! She gropes about under the bed*)
   Now, where is it?! (*She gropes and we hear an unmistakeable ping of
   china*) No, that's not it! Ah! 'Ere it is! (*She produces a bottle of gin. She
   sits on the side of the bed, empties the bottle in one go and smacks her lips*)
   This stuff won't cure a cold. But after a while you forget you've got the
   bloomin' thing! Oh, it's knocked me for six, this cold! I 'ope our Rosie got

my letter! I've been too weak to get to the shops. And there's some urgent supplies I'm in need of! (*She upturns the empty gin bottle and cackles. She thrusts the bottle back under the bed, again hitting the china*) Lummy! I think I've potted one!

There is a loud bang on the door

Oh, good! That'll be Rosie now! (*She clambers back into bed and calls out*) Come on in, me dear!

The door is pushed open. The Werewolf stands on the threshold

(*Peering across*) Come right in, lovie! No need to be shy with yer old Gran.

The Werewolf shambles in a little way

I've lost me dratted specs, so you'll 'ave to come closer, dear. Come on. Come and see Gran.

The Werewolf moves to the foot of the bed

(*Peering hard*) Crumbs! Our Rosie! You've filled out a bit since I last saw ya! I 'ope you're not takin' after yer mother!

The Werewolf gives a deep growl

And it sounds as if you've got a cold startin'. Oh, I've been proper poorly, Rosie. I 'aven't 'ad a morsel of food all day! Be a love an' make us a bacon butty, will ya? And fix yerself somethin' while you're at it. I expect you could do with a bite.

The Werewolf growls and nods its head. It rubs its belly hungrily. It picks up a large spotted handkerchief from the bed and ties it around its neck like a napkin. It advances on Grannie and stands right over her

(*Peering hard*) 'Ere, Rosie! I think it's time you paid a visit to [local hairdressers].

The Werewolf reaches out towards her. Grannie takes one of its claws and strokes it

And a little Immac wouldn't go amiss either, my girl! (*She gives an enormous sneeze and her glasses drop down on to her nose*) Ah! That's better... (*Sees the Werewolf looming over her*) No, it isn't! Aahhhgh!!

The Werewolf pounces on her, but she quickly rolls to one side and leaps out of bed. The Werewolf thrashes about on the bed, growling and snarling

Grannie is out of the door in a flash, slamming it shut behind her

The Werewolf howls in frustration and rips off the napkin. It spots the spare nightcap and snatches it up. Curiously, it looks at it, then puts it on its head. Comic business as it admires itself in the mirror on the wall DL. There is a knock at the door. The Werewolf reacts

Rosie (*off* C) Hallo, Grannie! It's me—Rosie!

The Werewolf gives a low growl and rubs its belly hungrily. Still wearing the nightcap, it jumps into the bed and pulls the covers up. The knock is repeated

(*Off* C) Can I come in, Grannie?

The Werewolf gives a growl that could be mistaken for "yes"

Rosie enters, closing the door behind her. She moves to the bed, concerned

Hallo, Grannie. How are you feeling?
Werewolf Ruff! Ruff!
Rosie Oh, dear! I'm sorry to hear that. Perhaps you should see a doctor.

The Werewolf growls in protest

But you sound so hoarse! (*She moves a little nearer*) Are you sure it's only a cold? You don't look yourself at all. What big eyes you have.
Werewolf (*in a growl*) All the better to see you with!
Rosie And what big ears you have.
Werewolf (*in a growl*) All the better to hear you with!
Rosie And what big teeth you have.
Werewolf (*in a growl*) All the better to—eat you with!! Gerrrah!! (*With a snarl, it springs up in bed and makes to grab for Rosie*)

She screams and rushes to the door. It is stuck! The Werewolf is out of bed in a flash and makes for her. Rosie runs away and seizes up the broom. The Werewolf lunges at her. She hits it on the head with the broom. With a whine, the Werewolf crashes to the floor, unconscious

The door bursts open and Roxie, Reggie and Grannie rush in. They see the prone Werewolf and react

Roxie Rosie!
Rosie (*quickly putting the broom against the wall*) I've only knocked it out!
Quick, Reggie! Run and fetch Count De Cash and the others!

No-one moves. They look at each other, uncomfortably

Well, what are you waiting for?! It could come round at any moment!
Roxie Er ... Rosie...
Rosie (*getting a bit annoyed*) What's the matter with you all?! Oh, I wish
Tom were here!
Reggie 'E *is*!!
Rosie (*eagerly looking towards the door*) Where?!
All Three (*pointing to the Werewolf*) There!!
Rosie (*nonplussed*) But ... what...
Roxie (*putting her arm around Rosie*) Rosie, my love. You've got to be very
brave. Prepare yerself for a shock. (*She points*) *That's* Tom! 'E's the
werewolf!
Rosie But... Oh, that's nonsense!
Reggie It's true, Rosie! We saw 'im change right in front of us!
Roxie One minute 'e was Mr Smoothie, the next [current hairy personality]!
Rosie (*looking at the Werewolf*) Tom?! ... Oh, Tom!! (*She cries and buries
her face in Roxie's bosom*)
Roxie And that's not all. 'E's not only a werewolf, 'e's...

Count De Cash enters through the doorway, followed by the Townsfolk

*They move down and react at seeing the Werewolf. Positions at this point
are—Werewolf on the floor* C. *Rosie and Family* R. *The Count* C. *The
Townsfolk* L

Count Excellent! Jolly good! You've caught the wetched cweature! Now
I'll finish it off with a silver bullet!

He and the Townsfolk aim their guns at the Werewolf. Rosie rushes across

Rosie No!! You mustn't kill him! You mustn't. It's Tom. We love each
other!

Reaction from the Townsfolk

Count (*lowering his pistol*) Weally? Is this twue?
Rosie & Family Yes!!
Count (*sounding as if he might change his mind*) Well, in that case...
(*Viciously*) Too bad! (*He pushes Rosie aside and aims his pistol again*)

Sternum rushes in, followed by Gertrude, Cringe and Cower

Sternum Stop!! You cannot kill that werewolf! He is Prince Rupert of
Pantovia!

*Sensation from the Townsfolk and they put up their muskets. Rosie is equally
shocked and looks at Roxie and Reggie. They nod*

Count It's… It's a lie.
Cringe Oh, no, it isn't! (*To Townsfolk*) 'E found out the Prince was a
werewolf and conned you lot into 'elpin' 'im kill it!
Cower Just so 'e could go on rulin' the country! 'E's a (*imitating the Count*)
wotton wascal!

Angry outcry from the Townsfolk directed at the Count

Count (*standing his ground*) Vewy well! But listen to me! What would you
have in my place, eh? (*Sneering*) A Pwince who changes into a savage
monster at every full moon and twies to eat people! Huh! Some wuler!
You're better off without him! Deny it if you can!

Murmurs of dissension from the Townsfolk

First Man I hate to admit it, but he's right!
First Woman Yes! Better the devil we know!
Second Man We can't be ruled by a werewolf!
All Townsfolk No! Death to the werewolf!!
Rosie (*desperately*) Wait! Wait! There must be a cure!
Count The only cure is with a silver bullet!
Townsfolk Aye!!

They aim their guns at the Werewolf

Grannie rushes across

Grannie Not so fast! 'Ang on a minute! Put them peashooters down!

They lower their guns

I know a rhyme!
Roxie Oh, Mum! This is no time for dirty ditties!
Grannie Not *that* sort of rhyme! It's about werewolves! My old Grannie
taught it to me when I was knee high to a grasshopper! Shh, all of you! Now,

'ow does it go? (*She recites*) "If a man be cursed by the werewolf's bane"...
er... (*Stumped*)

Reggie (*prompting*) Push him down the nearest drain?

Grannie No! No! "If a man be cursed by the werewolf's bane"... er...
(*Stumped again*)

Roxie (*prompting*) If 'e gets distemper 'e can't complain?

Grannie I've got it! I've got it! "If a man be cursed by the werewolf's *bane*—
a kiss from his true love will remove the curse and he'll never be a werewolf
ever—*again!*"

Roxie (*sarcastically*) Thank you, Sir John Bitumen!

Rosie Grannie, does that mean if I kiss the werewolf it will change back into
Tom?

Grannie Well, it's only an old rhyme, lovie—but it's worth a try!

Rosie (*to the others*) Shall I try it?

Others Yes!

Rosie (*to the audience*) Shall I?

"Yes!" from the audience

Count I think not!! (*He aims his pistol at the Werewolf*)

*Cringe and Cower quickly pounce on him and force the gun into the air. It
goes off with a loud bang. It would be nice if "plaster" fell from above! They
snatch the pistol away from the Count and hold him firmly between them*

Grannie (*looking up at the ceiling*) Charmin'! (*To the audience*) Now I'll
'ave to get [local odd job man or builders] in!

Cringe Go ahead, Rosie!

*Rosie hesitates, then kneels beside the Werewolf. Absolute stillness and quiet
from the others as she sings. Perhaps dim stage Lighting and bring up
spotlight on Rosie and Werewolf*

Song 12a—Reprise of Song 12

*After singing, Rosie leans forward and gently kisses the Werewolf. There is
a blinding flash, followed by a complete Black-out. Cries of alarm and
exclamations are heard during the Black-out*

*When the Lights come up, the Werewolf has gone and Prince Rupert lies
in its place—still wearing the nightcap! Delighted astonishment from
everyone—except Count De Cash of course*

Rosie (*overjoyed and hugging Grannie*) Oh, Grannie! It worked! It worked!

Rupert begins to stir. Rosie goes to him and helps him to sit up. He gazes about him in amazement

Rupert I... What's... (*Becoming aware of her*) Rosie!

They embrace. The Townsfolk sigh blissfully. Comic business as Rosie, Reggie and Grannie do a group hug. Gertrude hugs Sternum, Cringe and Cower squash the Count as they reach across to hug each other. Rupert, supported by Rosie, gets to his feet. He becomes aware of having a sore head and reaches up. He discovers the nightcap, takes it off and gazes at it in bewilderment

(*To Rosie*) I... I appear to have a sore head! How did I get that?
Rosie (*smiling*) *I* gave it to you, I'm afraid— (*she curtsies*) Your Royal Highness.

All the others bow and curtsy. Cringe and Cower force the Count to comply

Rupert (*reacting to the bowing*) I say! *Sternum!*
Sternum (*stepping forward*) Yes, Your Highness?
Rupert They all know who I am!
Sternum I regret to say it was unavoidable, Your Highness. (*He turns to Cringe and Cower*) I strongly suggest that you remove that miscreant and incarcerate him within the confines of a house of correction!
Cringe & Cower (*dumbly*) Pardon?
Sternum Bung 'im in the nick!
Cringe & Cower Right on!

Cringe and Cower drag the Count away. He sneers at the others and the audience as they exit UC, amid boos and hisses

Rupert (*totally confused by the whole proceedings*) I wish someone would tell me what's been going on! Why was I asleep on the floor—wearing this silly hat? What on earth has been happening?
Roxie Oh, just forget all about it, your Royal Flush!
Grannie Yes! Best to let *sleepin' dogs lie*! That's my motto!

The others agree. Rupert shrugs, then embraces Rosie. Everyone cheers. The music starts and they all go into a joyful song and dance

Song 13

After the song, a front-cloth is lowered or the tabs close

SCENE 6

Before the Royal Wedding

Tabs or the path front-cloth can be used. General Lighting

Reggie bounces on DR

Reggie (*waving to the audience*) Hallo, folks! Hi, kids! Well, that's it! It's all over! (*He sighs*) Aah! (*He encourages them to sigh "Aah" with him*) But it all ended happily, didn't it? That wotten wascal is in jail; where 'e belongs. Prince Rupert is back to normal, and he's gonna marry our Rosie! Mum's so excited about the wedding. She's already bought up all the hats in [local town]!

Roxie rushes on DL. *She wears an outrageous outfit that can be easily changed for the Finale*

Roxie Reggie! Reggie! Oh, there you are! I just can't make up me mind what to wear to the wedding! What would I look good in?
Reggie A mask? (*He guffaws*)

She takes a swing at him, but he ducks away

Roxie (*to the audience*) Oh, 'e's about as much use as chocolate tea pot! I've gotta look me best for the Royal Wedding, 'aven't I, folks? Got any suggestions what would show off my face an' figure?

Ad lib with the audience

Ooo! You *are* a rude lot! Just for that you're gonna 'ave to sing. Oh, yes! Not so clever now, are we! Thought you'd get away with it, didn't ya! We'll just sort out the words. (*To Reggie*) 'Ave you got the lyrics?
Reggie No, I always stand like this! (*He guffaws*)

She takes a swing at him, but misses. The song sheet is lowered or Reggie can fetch it from the wings. Comic business as they get the audience to sing. House Lights up. They can get children on to the stage

Song 14

After the song, the song sheet is removed. The children are given sweets and return to their seats. House Lights down

Roxie and Reggie wave goodbye to the audience and run out, as the Lights fade to Black-out

Music

SCENE 7

Grand Finale—The Royal Wedding

A special Finale setting, or the Town Square set can be used with flags and decorations, etc. Bright Lighting

Song 15

All enter singing for the Finale walkdown. The last to enter are Rosie and Rupert, magnificently attired

Rupert Our story is now over. T'was quite a hairy raising tale.

Cringe Not 'alf as hairy as *his* was when he was a giant Airedale!

Rosie My gallant Prince I've married. We'll never have a row.

Reggie 'E used to be a werewolf, but I think 'e's all right (*howling*) noooow!

Count My plans to wule the Countwy have gone to wack and wuin!

Cower They've banished 'im to [local place that fits the rhyme] for all 'is evil doin'!

Gertrude I've found my Mr Right at last, so 'appy we will be.

Sternum And if you get on *Countdown*, just ring the bell for me.

Roxie As mum-in-law to royalty, I'll 'ave to be refined! My prospects are enormous...

Reggie Especially from behind!

Grannie (*to Rosie*) I think you've grown a bit too old for my red riding hoods. Next year I'll give you vouchers for Marks or Littlewoods!

Werewolf At last I get a chance to speak, it makes a change from snarling. You see, I'm just an actor, but please don't call me darling!

Roxie You've all been such a lovely crowd, and acted as you should. There's nothing' more for us to say, except...

All Goodbye from *Little Red Riding Hood*!

Song 16

Final song. This can be a reprise

CURTAIN

FURNITURE AND PROPERTY LIST

Further dressing may be added at the director's discretion

ACT I

Scene 1

On stage: Town Square backcloth
Town Square wings
Roxie's house piece
"For Sale" and "To Let" signs
Street lamp

Off stage: Large paper bag containing picture frame with blank paper
backing (**Reggie**)
Parcel containing red riding hood (**Grannie**)
2 very large gift-wrapped boxes with false bottoms
(**Cringe** and **Cower**)

Personal: **Grannie:** walking stick, spectacles (throughout)
Count De Cash: handkerchief, quizzing glass (throughout)
Sternum: bowler hat, small salver with money bag

Scene 2

On stage: Path front cloth

Off stage: Basket (**Rosie**)
Basket (**Gertrude**)

Personal: **Cringe:** bag of sweets
Cower: bag of sweets

Scene 3

On stage: Room back wall with window
Room wings
Balloons and trimmings

"Happy Birthday Rosie" banner
Upright chairs

Personal: **All:** party hats

SCENE 4

On stage: Path front cloth

SCENE 5

On stage: As Act I, Scene 1

Off stage: Blunderbuss (**Roxie**)
Muskets (**Cringe**)
Muskets (**Cower**)

Personal: **Townsfolk:** nightcaps
Count De Cash: fancy pistol

ACT II

SCENE 1

On stage: Wood backcloth
Tree wings
Wood ground row
Cave entrance
Fallen tree trunk

Off stage: Muskets (**Chorus**)

Personal: **Roxie:** large handkerchief with hole
Reggie: large handkerchief in shreds
Count De Cash: pistol

SCENE 2

On stage: Dungeon front cloth
Small bench

Personal: **Count De Cash:** pistol

SCENE 3

On stage: As Act I, Scene 3 without decorations
               Large sofa

Off stage: Letter (**Rabbit**)
               Muskets (**Chorus**)
               Red riding hood (**SM**)

Personal: **Roxie:** whistle on ribbon
               Count De Cash pistol

SCENE 4

On stage: Path front cloth

Off stage: Muskets (**Chorus**)

Personal: **Count De Cash:** pistol
               Cower: large key

SCENE 5

On stage: Cottage room back wall flat with door
               Cottage wings
               Iron bedstead. *On it*: sheets, pillows, quilt, large spotted handkerchief,
                   nightcap. *Under it*: gin bottle, china pot
               Small table. *On it*: box of pills, medicine bottle
               Broom

Off stage: Muskets (**Chorus**)
               Duplicate nightcap (**Rupert**)

Personal: **Grannie:** spectacles, nightcap
               Count De Cash: pistol

SCENE 6

On stage: Path front cloth

Off stage: Song sheet (**Reggie** or **SM**)
               Sweets (**Roxie**)
               Sweets (**Reggie**)

SCENE 7

On stage: Special Finale set or Town Square
              Flags and bunting

Personal: **Werewolf:** large round "dog tag" with actor's name on it

LIGHTING PLOT

Practical fittings required: nil
Various interior and exterior settings

ACT I, SCENE 1

To open: General exterior lighting

Cue 1   Song 3 ends   (Page 16)
             Fade to black-out

ACT I, SCENE 2

To open: General exterior lighting

Cue 2   **Count De Cash** exits   (Page 21)
             Fade to black-out

ACT I, SCENE 3

To open: General interior lighting

Cue 3   **Rupert**: "I feel the same way"   (Page 25)
             Romantic lighting for duet

Cue 4   Song 7 ends   (Page 25)
             Return to general interior lighting

Cue 5   **Rupert**: "…important announcement to make!"   (Page 26)
             Full moon effect outside window

Cue 6   **Roxie**: "…sounds like 'e's found one!!"   (Page 27)
             Quick black-out

ACT I, SCENE 4

To open: Eerie lighting. Full moon on cloth

Cue 7   **Count De Cash** exits   (Page 32)
              Fade to black-out

ACT I, SCENE 5

To open: Eerie, moonlight effect

Cue 8   **Reggie**: "It's after me! Help!"   (Page 32)
              If possible, bring lights up in some windows

ACT II, SCENE 1

To open: Eerie, moonlight effect

Cue 9   **Werewolf** snores in cave, then silence   (Page 42)
              Fade to black-out

Cue 10   Dawn chorus of bird song   (Page 42)
              *Gradual effect of dawn coming up, into bright morning
                  sunshine*

Cue 11   End of reprise of No. 10 dance   (Page 45)
              Fade to black-out

ACT II, SCENE 2

To open: Gloomy interior lighting

Cue 12   **Gertrude**: "We need action!"   (Page 47)
              Follow spots on **Gertrude** *and* **Sternum**

Cue 13   Song 11 ends   (Page 47)
              Cut spots

Cue 14   **All**: "But how?!"   (Page 48)
              Quick black-out

ACT II, SCENE 3

To open: General interior lighting

Cue 15   **Roxie**: "And you lot at the back!"   (Page 50)
Bring up house lights

Cue 16   **Roxie**: "We ought to charge you extra!"   (Page 51)
Fade out house lights

Cue 17   **Rupert**: "…important announcement to make."   (Page 53)
Full moon effect outside window

Cue 18   **Roxie** and **Reggie** exit   (Page 56)
Quick black-out

ACT II, SCENE 4

To open: Eerie lighting. Full moon on cloth

Cue 19   **Rosie**: "Oh, Tom! Where are you?"   (Page 56)
Spot on **Rosie** *as she sings*

Cue 20   Song 12 ends   (Page 56)
Cut spots

Cue 21   **Roxie** exits   (Page 59)
Fade to black-out

ACT II, SCENE 5

To open: General interior lighting

Cue 22   **Rosie** kneels beside the **Werewolf**   (Page 64)
Dim lighting and bring up spot on **Rosie** *and* **Werewolf**

Cue 23   **Rosie** kisses **Werewolf**   (Page 64)
Flash, followed by complete black-out. Allow time for
    Rupert *to change places with* **Werewolf**, *then return*
    to general interior lighting

Lighting Plot   75

ACT II, Scene 6

To open: General lighting

Cue 24   **Roxie** and **Reggie** get children from audience   (Page 66)
            Bring up house lights

Cue 25   **Children** return to their seats   (Page 66)
            Take down house lights

Cue 26   **Roxie** and **Reggie** exit   (Page 67)
            Fade to black-out

ACT II, Scene 7 (Finale)

To open: Bright general lighting

No cues

EFFECTS PLOT

ACT I

ACT II

MADE AND PRINTED IN GREAT BRITAIN BY
LATIMER TREND & COMPANY LTD PLYMOUTH
MADE IN ENGLAND